Program Authors

Lindamichelle Baron • Sharon Sicinski-Skeans

Modern Curriculum Press

Parsippany, New Jersey

Special thanks to the following schools for providing student writing samples:

Allendale Elementary School
Oakland, CA

Barbara Bush Elementary School,
Houston, TX

Camden Elementary School, Camden, NJ

Center Ridge Elementary School
Centreville, VA

Chattanooga School for Arts and Science
Chattanooga, TN

Clinton Elementary School
Maplewood, NJ

Glenwood Elementary School
Short Hills, NJ

Jackson School, Des Moines, IA

Kennedy Elementary School
Santa Ana, CA

Roy Allen Elementary School
Melbourne, FL

Steelton-Highspire Elementary School
Steelton, PA

Wadsworth Elementary School
Chicago, IL

Weslaco ISD
Weslaco, TX

William Halley Elementary School
Fairfax Station, VA

Winston Churchill School
Fairfield, NJ

Project Editor: *Betsy Niles* • Designers: *Karolyn Wehner, Lisa Arcuri, Steve Barth, Dorothea Fox & Michelle Episcopo*
Cover Design: *Senja Lauderdale & Chris Otazo* • Cover Illustration: *Bernard Adnet*

Acknowledgments

"Basketball Star" from *My Daddy is a Cool Dude and Other Poems* by Karama Fufuka. Copyright © 1975 by Karama Fufuka. Reprinted by permission of Dial Books for Young Readers, a division of Penguin Putnam Inc.

"The Fox and the Crow" from *The Best of Aesop's Fables* by Margaret Clark. Illustrated by Charlotte Voake. Text copyright © 1990 by Margaret Clark. Illustration copyright © 1990 by Charlotte Voake. Reprinted by permission of Little, Brown and Company.

"Have A Balloon Blowout" by Julie Vosburgh Agnone from *National Geographic World Magazine*. Copyright © 1998 National Geographic Society. Text and cover reprinted by permission of National Geographic Society.

"Ekatarina Gordeeva Milk Mustache Ad" and "Patrick Ewing Milk Mustache Ad" Copyright © 1998 by National Fluid Milk Processor Promotion Board. Reprinted by permission of Bozell Worldwide, Inc.

"National Aquarium in Baltimore" brochure reprinted by permission of the National Aquarium in Baltimore.

"Picturing the World" by Allison Lassieur from *Highlights for Children*. Copyright © 1997 by Highlights for Children, Inc., Columbus, Ohio. Text and cover reprinted by permission of Highlights for Children.

Racing the Sun by Paul Pitts. Copyright © 1988 by Paul Pitts. Text and cover reprinted by permission of Avon Books, Inc. and The Ray Peekner Literary Agency.

Uncle Phil's Diner by Helena Clare Pittman. Copyright © 1998 by Carolrhoda Books, Inc. Used by permission of the publisher. All rights reserved.

"Dictionary entry" from *Webster's New World Dictionary for Explorers of Language*. Copyright © 1991 by Simon & Schuster. Reprinted with permission of Modern Curriculum Press.

Cursive font used by permission of Zaner-Bloser, Inc.

Art and photo credits appear on page 282.

Modern Curriculum Press

An imprint of Pearson Learning
299 Jefferson Road, P.O. Box 480, Parsippany, NJ 07054-0480
www.pearsonlearning.com
1-800-321-3106

ISBN: 0-7652-0750-8

4 5 6 7 8 9 10   RRD   07 06 05 04 03 02 01 00

Contents

Get Ready to Write

The Process of Writing

The Forms of Writing

Writer's Handbook

GET READY TO WRITE

Book Tour—A Quick Look

How can this book help me become a better writer?

The Write Direction is full of great ideas about writing. It helps you get started on a new writing project. It shows you how to be a better writer, and it can help you when you have questions. Many of the writing samples were written by real kids just like you. So, if they can write, you can, too!

The book is divided into four main sections:

Get Ready to Write

The first unit gets you thinking about writing and how to go about doing it.

The Process of Writing

This unit introduces you to the five different stages of the writing process: prewriting, drafting, revising, editing and proofreading, and publishing.

The Forms of Writing

You always write for a reason. This unit shows you different kinds of writing. Some you already know. Others will be new to you. You can go back to this section for help with all your writing projects.

Writer's Handbook

The first part of this section, Writer's Craft, shows you how to make your writing more interesting. The second part is a guide to using correct grammar, punctuation, and spelling.

Are there any special features in the book to help me?

You'll find six special features scattered throughout *The Write Direction*. Look through the book. Can you find examples of each one?

Your Turn gives you a chance to use what you have just learned. You learn to write by writing. Step-by-step directions make writing easy and fun.

Think Like a Writer ★ These questions will get you thinking like a writer.

Become a Super Writer

You can turn to the *Writer's Handbook* section when you need help with writing and language skills.

Tech Tip Here are some hints for using a computer to write. Learn to let your computer do the work for you.

Writer's Tip Stuck? Here are suggestions to help you become a better writer.

Get to know your book!

You don't need a compass to find your way around this book. All you need is the table of contents and the index. Use them to answer these questions.

On which page will you find

- how to write a realistic story?
- what *exaggeration* means?
- where to put a comma?

Now you're going in *The Write Direction!*

Portfolio This feature will help you get organized by reminding you how and when to save your work.

Writing to Learn

You are learning all the time.

From the time you wake up in the morning until you go to bed at night, you are learning. You learn at home, in school, and by exploring the world around you. You learn by . . .

READING WATCHING DOING LISTENING

You also learn by writing. When you write down information, you can read it and think about the ideas.

Writing helps you

- remember important information.
- organize your ideas.
- make a plan.
- ask questions when you need more information.

> I have a special notebook where I write things I want to remember.

Science Experiment

Growing radish seeds

Bring in
  1. radish seeds
  2. small dish
  3. paper towel
  4. plastic wrap

Notes

September 21, 1999

Today we went to the new aquarium in the city. I liked the penguins best. When they swim underwater, they look more like fish than birds.

Journal Entry

Think Like a Writer

★ How do you remember important things?

★ What kind of writing helps you learn?

Writing to Tell a Story

What kind of stories do you like?

There are so many kinds of stories, it's hard to choose. Do you like animal stories, fairy tales, or scary mysteries? Stories can be about almost anything. The one thing they have in common is that they are fun to read—and write.

How does a writer tell an entertaining story?

Think about what you like most about the stories you read. What keeps you reading?

Clues and suspense make a mystery exciting. Realistic stories need interesting characters and a problem for the hero to solve. All well-written stories have a beginning, a middle, and an end.

Here are the beginnings of two kinds of stories. One story could be real, and the other is make-believe.

We seemed to drive forever. Then we turned a corner, and there it was—the Parkside Animal Shelter. We were going to get a dog—my very own dog! . . .
Personal Narrative

A long time ago, in a faraway land, a dragon walked through the forest, looking for trouble. He was a fire-breathing dragon with shiny green scales . . .
Fantasy

Think Like a Writer
★ Whom are you writing for? Your friends, your family, your teacher?
★ What do they enjoy reading about?

Writing to Describe

How do you get others to see what you see?

You could draw a picture. You could make a video with music and sound.

You could also use words to tell about what you see.

How do you write a description?

Describing is giving a picture of something in words. You can describe something by telling

- how it looks, sounds, feels, tastes, and smells.
- how it makes you feel.
- what it reminds you of.
- how it is similar to something else.

Here are two descriptions. After you read them, close your eyes and try to see what the writer saw.

My favorite place is the playground. It's like being in the circus.
On the rings I'm an acrobat flying through the air . . .

Comparison

I make my favorite place with a chair, a table, and a blanket. It's a tent in the hot desert. It's a cave in the ice. It's a submarine under the sea. It's whatever I want it to be. It's my imagination.

Description

Think Like a Writer

★ What special person or place would you like to describe?

★ What are some words you could use in your description?

Writing to Inform

Information, please!

How tall is a giraffe? Where is the rain forest? Who holds the home-run record in baseball? When you want information, you can look it up in an encyclopedia, read a book, ask a teacher, or search the Internet.

Do you have a subject that you know a lot about? Then you too are a source for information. When you write to inform, you give readers facts and information.

What do your readers want to know about?

Topics that interest you will probably interest your readers. Your topic can be something you already know a lot about or something you want to learn more about. The more interested you are in a topic, the more you will enjoy writing about it.

Both a how-to paragraph and a report give the reader information about a subject.

To make pancakes, you add milk and eggs to pancake mix. Stir the batter until it is smooth. Then pour a spoonful of batter onto a hot griddle. In a minute or two your pancakes will be ready.

How-to Paragraph

Did you know that the cheetah is the fastest animal on four legs? It can run up to 70 miles an hour. That's faster than most cars drive on the highway. The fastest a person can run is only 28 miles an hour . . . .

Information Report

Think Like a Writer

★ How do you know if you've given your readers enough information?

Writing to Persuade

How do you get others to agree with you?

You could try having a temper tantrum. It didn't work very well when you were little, so it probably won't work now. Explaining why you feel the way you do would probably work better.

When you want other people to see things your way, you need to give them reasons why they should agree with you.

How do you write to persuade others?

Look through a magazine or a newspaper. What do you see? The advertisements, letters to the editor, and movie reviews are all examples of using writing to persuade.

In the models below, both writers have good reasons for their points of view. Do you agree with them?

I really enjoyed <u>Cloudy With a Chance of Meatballs</u>. I think it's a great idea to have a place where food falls out of the sky and no one needs to cook. I loved this book. You will, too.

Book Review

Dear Dad,
    Remember that bicycle we talked about? Here are some important things to think about. My bike is too small. I've earned half of the money to pay for a new one. I can ride to school every day, so I'll never be late. What do you say?

            Love,
            Jenna

                Letter

Think Like a Writer

★ What type of writing will make readers see things your way?

Writing for Yourself and Others

Who will read your writing?

There are some kinds of writing that are just for you. They have "Private—Keep Out" written all over them.

- an entry in your diary
- a note you write to yourself

You write for yourself when you want to remember things or express yourself. You may also want to sort out your feelings or think something through.

Some writing you do to share your ideas with others. Writing is also an important part of your schoolwork.

- homework
- logs
- book reports
- stories and poems

The diary entry below is an example of writing for yourself. A poem is one kind of writing you share.

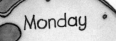

Monday

Dear Diary,
I can't believe I've grown a whole inch. I'm not the shortest one in the class anymore. Maybe now I can play basketball. I just hope I keep growing.

Diary Entry

My Favorite Pet

Fish make the best pets.
Now I'll tell you why.
Clown fish make me laugh
And angel fish can fly.

Poem

Think Like a Writer ★ What kind of writing do you like to share with other people?

Planning Your Portfolio

What's a portfolio?

Do you ever look at your baby pictures? How could you ever have been so small? You've grown a lot since then. A portfolio is like a photo album. It's a collection of your writing that lets you see how much you've grown as a writer.

A portfolio can be anything you keep your writing in—a folder, a notebook, or even a box. Your portfolio helps you organize your writing. You can reread your favorite pieces and share them with others. More important, you will see how the writing process has helped you become a better writer.

What do you keep in your portfolio?

Every time you write, you make a stack of paper. You have prewriting notes and more than one draft. You have a final clean copy. You may even have a picture or two. With so many pieces of paper, it's easy to misplace something important.

Portfolio

Throughout this book you'll find the Portfolio logo. It will remind you to save your writing.

A portfolio can help you organize your papers.

My Portfolio

For each writing project, you will probably have the following papers.

- a list of brainstorming ideas
- prewriting notes
- pictures, charts, or drawings, like the cluster diagram below
- your drafts with changes marked on them
- your final copy

Keep all of these together in your portfolio. When it's time to write, you can get right to work.

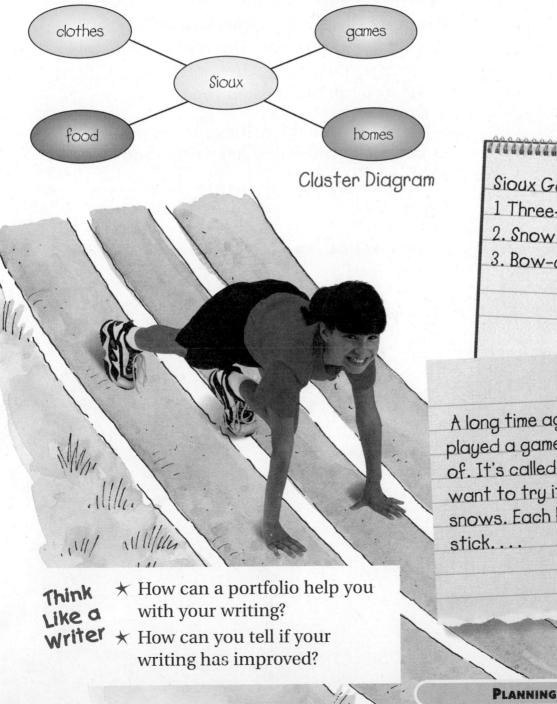

clothes

games

Sioux

food

homes

Cluster Diagram

Sioux Games
1 Three-Mile Race
2. Snow Snake
3. Bow-and-Arrow Race

Notes

A long time ago, Sioux children played a game I'd never heard of. It's called Snow Snake. I want to try it as soon as it snows. Each kid had a long stick. . . .

Draft

Think Like a Writer
★ How can a portfolio help you with your writing?
★ How can you tell if your writing has improved?

How do you make your own portfolio?

Although a portfolio can be anything that keeps your writing together in one place, your teacher will probably want you to use some kind of folder. You can make a writing portfolio in different ways.

- Use a ready-made folder with pockets.
- Make a folder from two sheets of thin cardboard. Tape or staple together three sides. Then slip your papers in through the open side.
- Decorate your portfolio with paint, markers, stickers, or glitter.

Your teacher will make a special place in the classroom to store everyone's portfolios. Remember to put your portfolio back when you're done with it. That way, you can find it when you need it.

Think Like a Writer ★ How can the writing in your portfolio help you with other writing you do?

How can you organize the writing in your portfolio?

With so much paper, you'll need to keep your portfolio organized. A table of contents can help you keep track of the different writing projects you've done over the year. Here's one you can use as a model. It can be written on paper or on the inside front cover of your folder or on a separate sheet of paper.

My Table of Contents

Title	Prewriting Date	Publishing Date
Sparky Goes to the Pet Fair	September 14	September 28
Report on Sioux Games	November 3	November 21
Book report on Little House on the Prairie	December 1	December 16

Where do you keep your best writing?

Sometimes your teacher may ask you to keep a special portfolio of your best writing. Your teacher will use this writing to see how your work has improved.

Your Turn

First, make and decorate your portfolio. Then you can make a table of contents.

- Use a clean sheet of white paper to make a table of contents.
- Use the headings in the table of contents shown here or headings your teacher suggests.
- Each time you start a new writing project, add it to your table of contents along with the date.

Paper, Pen, and Word Processing

Writing by hand

For Your First Draft

- Use lined yellow paper to show that it's a work in progress.
- Write on every other line. Leave yourself space to make changes.
- Write on one side of the paper only. You might want to cut and paste.

> When I write my draft, I leave room to make changes.

Desert Plants

Plants have unusual ways

of adapting to the hot, dry climate

of the (dessert) the desert saguaro

cactus has a large, thick stem. . .

First Draft

Desert Plants
Plants have unusual ways of adapting to the hot, dry climate of the desert. The saguaro cactus has a large, thick stem that can hold many gallons of water!

Final Copy

> When I write my final copy, I use my best handwriting.

For Your Final Copy

- Use lined white paper to show that it's your final copy.
- Start on the top line. Leave a one-inch margin on the sides and bottom.
- Use your best printing. Use cursive script if your teacher tells you to.
- Be neat. If the paper starts to look smudged or messy, start over again.
- Use your imagination to make a cover.

Think Like a Writer

★ Why do clear handwriting and a neat paper make your writing easier to read?

★ How do you feel about your writing?

Writing on a computer

A computer can make writing easier, faster, and more fun. You just need to know a few basic commands to get started. Look for the words *File, Edit,* and *Tools* at the top of your screen.

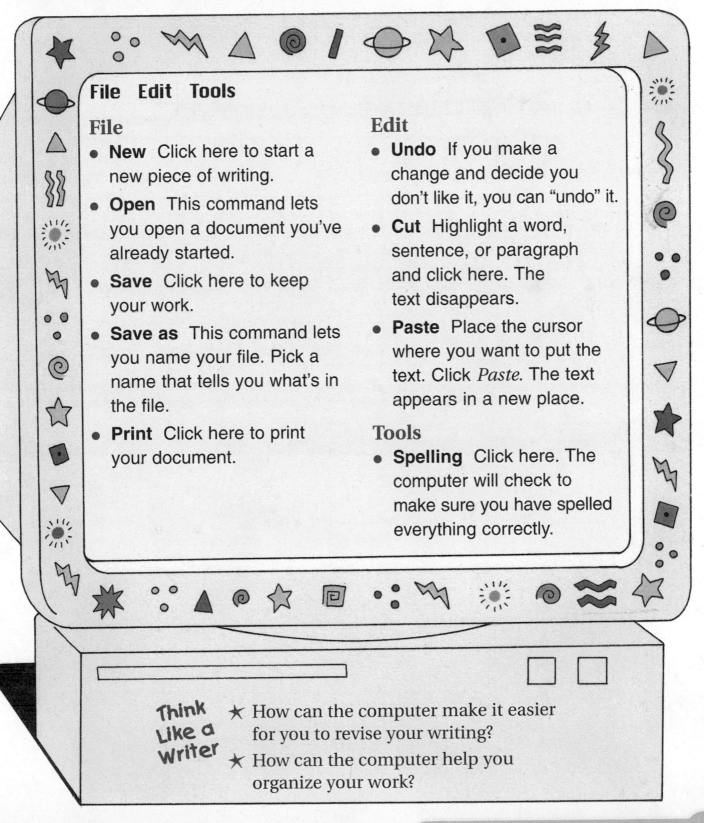

File   Edit   Tools

File

- **New** Click here to start a new piece of writing.
- **Open** This command lets you open a document you've already started.
- **Save** Click here to keep your work.
- **Save as** This command lets you name your file. Pick a name that tells you what's in the file.
- **Print** Click here to print your document.

Edit

- **Undo** If you make a change and decide you don't like it, you can "undo" it.
- **Cut** Highlight a word, sentence, or paragraph and click here. The text disappears.
- **Paste** Place the cursor where you want to put the text. Click *Paste.* The text appears in a new place.

Tools

- **Spelling** Click here. The computer will check to make sure you have spelled everything correctly.

Think Like a Writer
- ★ How can the computer make it easier for you to revise your writing?
- ★ How can the computer help you organize your work?

THE PROCESS OF WRITING

The Stages in the Process

Writing is something we do every day. We write notes to ourselves. We write letters and E-mail to other people. We also write stories and reports.

When we write, we also think and plan and change our writing to make it better. Here are the stages that most writers follow in the process of writing.

> Follow these five stages, and you'll be a star writer!

1. Prewriting

Prewriting is planning and getting ready to write.

- Brainstorm to get ideas.
- Select a topic.
- Gather information.
- Make a writing plan.
- Decide what to say and how to say it.

5. Publishing

Publishing is sharing your work with others. There are many ways to publish your writing.

- Write a paper.
- Send a letter or an E-mail.
- Make a book.
- Tell a story.
- Put on a play.

2. Drafting

Drafting is putting your ideas on paper.

- Use your writing plan as a guide.
- Let your ideas flow onto the paper.
- Don't stop to fix mistakes in spelling or grammar.

Think Like a Writer ★ Follow the red arrows. What do they tell you?

3. Revising

Revising is changing and improving your writing.

- Read over your writing.
- Make sure you followed your writing plan.
- Add, move, or take out information and ideas.

4. Editing and Proofreading

Editing and proofreading is giving your work a final check. Read your revised work carefully. Look for mistakes in

- Grammar
- Capitalization
- Punctuation
- Spelling

Then proofread your work one last time to catch any mistakes you might have missed.

 **Prewriting**

Think It Through

Prewriting is the beginning of the writing process. In this stage, writers gather information and make a plan for their work. Prewriting is a time for thinking and making choices.

Brainstorming

Brainstorming is a special way of thinking. It is an important part of prewriting.

When you brainstorm, one idea leads to another . . . and another . . . and another. In almost no time at all, you have a topic to write about.

There are many ways to brainstorm. Here are a few.

- Make a list of things that you've done or that you know about.

- Do a quick write. Write down everything you know about a topic. Keep writing until you run out of ideas.

- Talk with other people to get ideas.

Story Ideas
1. Soccer
2. Animals
✔ 3. My dog

Books!

Select a Topic

Brainstorming will give you many ideas to write about. Ask yourself these questions.

- Which topic do I like best?
- Which topic do I know the most about?
- Which topic will other people want to read about?

Conferencing

There's nothing like putting another mind to work on a problem. In conferencing, you meet with a partner or in a small group to talk about your writing.

Gather Information

For just about any kind of writing, you need to gather facts and details about your subject.

- Read books, magazines, and newspapers.
- Search the Internet.
- Talk to people.

Think Like a Writer

★ What are some other ways to get ideas for writing?
★ How can you keep track of all your ideas?

MAGAZINES!

NEWSPAPERS!

Organize Your Information

Once you have answered your questions, you need to organize the information you have found. One of the best ways is to put the information in a diagram or chart.

Cluster Diagram

Comparison Chart

KWL (Know-Want-Learn) Chart

Think Like a Writer

★ Why do you think writers ask themselves questions that tell *who, what, when, where,* and *how?*

★ Which chart works better for writing a story?

Design a Plan

Now that you know your topic and have some information, it's time to make a writing plan. A writing plan tells you what to write and how to organize it.

There are different ways to make a writing plan. Choose one that works with the kind of writing you're doing. Here are some examples.

Subject—What am I writing about?

Purpose—Why am I writing?

Audience—Who will read my writing?

Form—What kind of writing will this be?

Beginning
Introduce main characters, setting, and plot.

Middle
Tell what happened in the order it happened.

End
Tell how everything works out.

Story Map

When You Conference

If you are the writer,

- don't be afraid to ask for help.
- ask questions about how you can improve your writing.
- listen carefully to your partner's suggestions.

If you are helping a writer,

- point out what is good about a piece of writing.
- if asked, give examples of how the writing can be improved.
- be positive.

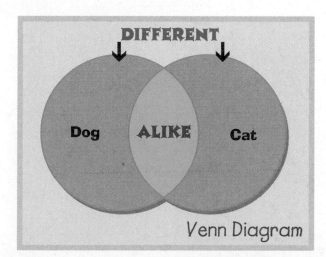

Venn Diagram

Drafting Put It Into Words

In prewriting, you chose a topic, gathered information, and made a plan for your writing. Now you're ready for the next stage in the process—drafting, or writing. Writing a draft

- helps get your ideas onto the page.
- lets you try out many different ideas and words.
- gives you a chance to make changes.

Write a First Draft

How do you begin your draft? Start by looking at your writing plan. Get your ideas organized in your head. Then start writing. Don't worry about spelling or grammar. Just get your ideas on paper.

As you're writing, look back at your writing plan. This will help you keep your ideas in order.

Writer's Tip
When you write a first draft, write on every other line. This gives you room to make changes.

Sparky Goes to the Pet Fair
I. How Paul Got Sparky
  A. Paul Wants a Dog
  B. A Trip to the Animal Shelter
II. Paul Trains Sparky
  A. Sparky Learns to Play Catch

Outline

Sparky Goes to the Pet Fair

Paul and his family went to the animal shelter. Paul's friend had gotten a cat from the shelter last year. They saw every kind of dog you could imagine. Then they saw Sparky. Sparky had a short tail.

When they got home, Paul wanted to teach Sparky some tricks.

Draft

Audience

As you write your first draft, think about your subject and audience. Your audience is who you are writing for. It could be your teacher, family, friends, or yourself.

Ask yourself these questions.

- What would my readers like to learn?
- What would my readers enjoy?

Purpose

Your purpose is the reason you are writing. You might want to write because

- you miss your best friend who moved away.
- you want to share something funny.

Writer's Tip
Try to picture your reader in your mind. This will help you decide if your writing is right for your audience.

Form

Form is the kind of writing you do. It should match your purpose and audience. For example, you might write

- a letter to a friend who has moved.
- a story about something funny that happened.

Conferencing

Meeting with a partner can be a big help when you're writing a draft. If you get stuck and don't know what to write next, your partner might have some ideas.

Revising Take Another Look

Can you imagine what life would be like if you got another chance at everything you did? If you were playing baseball and struck out, you'd get another time at bat. When someone offered you a plate of cookies, if you didn't like your first choice, you could have another—without even asking!

Revising is the third stage of the writing process. In this stage you get a second chance. Actually, you get as many chances as you need to change and to improve your writing.

Unimportant information is deleted.

Descriptive words make writing more interesting.

Sparky Goes to the Pet Fair

Paul and his family went to the animal

shelter. ~~Paul's friend had gotten a cat from~~

~~the shelter last year~~. They saw every kind

of dog you could imagine. Then they saw

brown ears and

Sparky. Sparky had a short brown tail.

When they got home, Paul wanted to

teach Sparky some tricks.

Information

The first step in revising is to check your information. Use your notes and writing plan to be sure that

- all your facts are correct.
- you have included all the information your readers need.
- you have taken out any information you don't really need.

Writer's Tip
When you revise, make your changes right on your first draft. Don't forget to use revising marks.

Organization

Next check the order, or organization, of your writing. Ask yourself the following questions.

- Did I tell things in the order that they happened?
- Does my writing have a beginning, a middle, and an end?
- Did I put important facts first? Do I have enough details to explain them?

Language

Revising also gives you a second chance to improve the language of your work. Think carefully about the words you have used. Do they say exactly what you want? What could you do to make them more interesting?

Start at the beginning and go through your work word by word. What words could you use to make your writing more interesting or easier to understand? Use words that will help your readers see, hear, smell, taste, or even feel what you are describing.

Conferencing

If you can, conference with a partner or small group when you revise. Read your draft aloud and ask your partner for ideas and suggestions. Ask the following questions.

- Is my main idea clear?
- Did I tell things in the right order?
- Is there anything else I need to add?
- Are there better words I could have used?

Think Like a Writer

★ What words can you use to make the order of events clearer?
★ How can you make your writing more interesting?

Did I leave anything out?

Polish Your Writing

The writing process not only gives you a second chance to review your work, it also gives you a third! The editing and proofreading stage is your chance to put the finishing touches on your writing—to check your grammar, punctuation, capitalization, and spelling.

When you edit and proofread, you read your writing again . . . and again. Each time you read it, look for a different kind of mistake.

> **Writer's Tip**
> The Writer's Handbook section is a good place to get help with grammar and usage skills.

Grammar

The rules that tell you how to speak and write correctly are called *grammar*. For example, the subject and the verb in a sentence must agree.

Janet **hits** the ball.

Dave and Jim **hit** the ball, too.

Usage

Grammar gives you the rules for using language. *Usage* is the way you use words in sentences. For example, the word *good* is an adjective. The word *well* is an adverb. They are used differently.

Paul is a good student.

He does well on tests.

Think Like a Writer

★ How can reading your work aloud help you find mistakes in your writing?

Mechanics

Read your writing again. Look for mistakes in capitalizing letters, punctuating sentences, and spelling words.

Capitalization

Check for words that should begin with capital letters. Here are some words you should check.

- Names   Chris Jackson
- Titles   Dr. Amy Glass
- Months   December
- Days   Monday

Punctuation

Punctuation is how you use periods, commas, question marks, exclamation marks, apostrophes, and quotation marks to make your writing clear.

- Does every sentence end with a period, question mark, or exclamation mark?

- Did you put commas in dates, addresses, and words in a series?

Spelling

Once you have checked and corrected any punctuation errors in your work, read it over for spelling mistakes.

- Check the spelling of any words that are new or that you know give you trouble.

- Use the **Writer's Handbook** section of this book, a dictionary, or the spelling tool on your computer to help you.

- Keep a personal spelling dictionary in the language arts section of your Learning Log to help you learn new or difficult words.

Appearance

After you edit and proofread your work, take time to make a neat, final copy.

- Don't leave out any words or skip any of the changes you have decided to make.

- If you are writing by hand, use your best penmanship.

- If you are using a computer, make sure things look correct on the screen before you print your work.

Think Like a Writer

★ How can the **Writer's Handbook** and a dictionary help with this stage of the writing process?

Proofreading Marks

Mark	Meaning
¶	indent first line of paragraph
≡	capitalize
∧ or ∨	add
℘	remove
⊙	add a period
/	make lowercase
◯	spelling mistake
⌒	move
∾	transpose

Tech Tip

Most word-processing programs have a spell-checking tool that will help you find errors.

Share Your Work

Are you ready for some fun? The last stage of the writing process is publishing. This is your chance to share your writing with your friends and family.

When you think of publishing, you probably think of books. That's a good start. There are many creative ways to publish your work.

In Print

Books

It's easy to make your writing into a book. All you have to do is fasten the pages together and put a cover around them. It's just a matter of knowing what kind of book you want to make. Here are a few ideas.

- **Shape book**—Cut out the pages of your book in the shape of the subject of your writing.

- **Anthology**—Collect your favorite poems or stories, illustrate them, and publish them together.

- **Picture book**—Illustrate one of your stories and make it into a book for younger children to read.

Sparky Goes to the Pet Fair

Paul and his family went to the animal shelter. They saw every kind of dog you could imagine. Then they saw Sparky. Sparky had brown ears and a short brown tail.

When they got home, Paul wanted to teach Sparky some tricks. Paul took Sparky to the park where he taught him to catch a ball.

Magazines and Newspapers

A class magazine or newspaper is a great way to share your writing. Have classmates contribute a favorite piece of writing. Add some illustrations and give a copy to everyone in the school.

Displays

Show your work on a bulletin board in the classroom or in the hall. Add pictures, photos, or charts to make it interesting. Give the display a title.

Illustrations, Charts, and Graphs

- **Illustrations**—Pictures and photos make stories and poems more fun to read.
- **Charts**—Tables and lists help organize information for your reader.
- **Graphs**—Remember these from math class? Graphs show how the numbers or amounts of things are related to each other.

Tech Tip
Most writing programs are easy to use. You don't have to know everything before you begin.

Using Computers

How did you ever write without one? Not only do computers make writing easy, but they also help make your writing look good. You can
- use different sizes and styles of type.
- make headlines and borders.
- add art, charts, and graphs.

In Person

Not all writing ends up on a printed page. Sometimes the best way to share your writing is to tell it in person.

Stories and Poems

A great way to share your stories and poems is to read them aloud. Since you wrote the story, you can make the characters come alive.

Oral Reports and Speeches

When you give an oral report or a speech, you talk directly to your audience. You give them information or try to get them to agree with you. Afterward, your audience can ask you questions.

On Tape

Maybe you would prefer to act out a story, poem, or play. Put on a play and videotape it. Recite a poem and tape-record it. Music, costumes, and scenery will make your performance complete.

Think Like a Writer

★ What other ways can you think of to publish your writing?

THE FORMS OF WRITING

TAKE NOTE

Writing to Learn

Notes

Writing Notes

Notes can help you remember an important telephone message, your cat's birthday, or what you need for tomorrow's science project. Notes can also help you learn. As you read, pick out the important facts and write them down. Later, your notes will help you remember what you've studied.

MCP Science, page 12

Constellation — a group of stars
   that form a pattern

88 constellations

form a map of the sky
   that helps astronomers

Talk About the Model

★ How does the writer know where the information came from?

★ What facts does the writer want to remember?

Take notes on several pages in your science or social studies book.

- First, write down the book title and page number so you'll remember where the information came from.

- Next, write down the topic.

- Then, list only the important facts in each paragraph.

- You can write just a few words or whole sentences.

- Reread your notes to be sure they are clear and have enough information.

Meet the Writer

I took these notes when we studied the solar system in science. I wrote down just the important facts. My notes will help me remember what I read.

Joey Tan
Pennsylvania

Writing Lists

You can make **lists** of things to do and lists of things you've seen. Making lists can help you learn. They can help you organize your thoughts and remember important facts and ideas.

Meet the Writer

Lists help me get ideas for my writing. I'm writing about my parakeet, so I made a list of all the things I wanted to include. I can add to it later.

Emily Barton
Mississippi

My Parakeet
1. color
2. wings and feathers
3. food
4. toys
5. tricks I taught him
6. words he can say

Talk About the Model

★ What else could the writer add to her list?

★ Why did the writer number the items in her list?

★ How can writing lists help you in school?

Your Turn

Lists can help you remember important information. They can also help you when you write.

- Look through your journal.
- Choose a topic that interests you.
- Make a list of things you could write about your topic.
- You may wish to number the items in your list.
- When you finish, exchange lists with a partner and compare them.

Writing Log Entries

A **log** is a notebook where you can write notes, ideas, and questions about things you learn. There are three kinds of logs that can help you learn. In a Literature Log, you write about the books you read. In a Learning Log, you write about the subjects you study in school, and in an Observation Log, you write about the things you see around you.

Literature Log

A **Literature Log** can help you remember all your favorite books. It's a good place to get ideas for writing your own stories.

> February 26
>
> What's the Matter With
> Herbie Jones?
> by Suzy Kline
> Herbie and his friend Raymond act like me and my friend Josh. Herbie often gets into trouble, just as I do, but Raymond is there to help him. The story made me think about how important it is to have friends.
> Maybe I'll write a story about Josh and me.

Literature Log | Learning Log | Observation Log

Meet the Writer

I use one notebook and divide it into three sections, one for each kind of log.

Julian Little
Georgia

I'm Julian. This is my friend Josh.

Talk About the Model

★ Why is it important to include the title and author of the books in your Literature Log?

★ Why did the writer write about this book in his Literature Log?

Learning Log

In a **Learning Log,** you write about social studies, science, math, and language arts. It's a good place to ask questions about things you don't understand and things you want to know more about.

Literature Log

Learning Log

Observation Log

April 15

Independence Day

On July 4, 1776, the United States of America became a nation. Every year since then, we have celebrated Independence Day. There are different ways to celebrate. People often have picnics, parades, and fireworks. Many people fly our nation's flag outside their houses.

What does <u>independence</u> mean?

Talk About the Model

★ Why does the writer ask a question at the end of the entry?

★ How can writing in a log help the writer learn?

Observation Log

Carry your **Observation Log** with you. Write quickly so that you don't miss anything. Sometimes, drawing a picture can help you describe what you see.

October 12

Literature Log

Learning Log

Observation Log

Class Trip to the Zoo

The giraffes are standing together across the field. They're busy eating leaves off the trees. They don't make any noise. Suddenly, one starts to run toward us. It comes right up to the fence and looks down at me. Up close it's huge! I never thought a giraffe could be that tall!

I wonder how tall it is?

Talk About the Model

★ What else could the writer have told about the giraffes?

★ How can the writer use this information later?

Make your own logs. Get a notebook and divide it into three main sections, using paper or plastic tabs. Label the tabs Literature Log, Learning Log, and Observation Log. Then divide the Learning Log into sections, one for each subject.

- Put the date at the beginning of each entry.

- Write down all the facts and information you want to remember.

- Ask questions about things you don't understand.

Writer's Tip
Writing in a log every day makes it easy to put your thoughts into words.

Writing Journal Entries

Meet the Writer

I write in my journal every day. I write about things that happen at home or in school. Sometimes, I write a lot and sometimes I only write a few sentences.

Gina
Bonsecour
Maine

What would you keep in a scrapbook— pictures of friends, postcards from vacation, a first-place ribbon from the science fair? A scrapbook is a place to keep things you want to remember.

Writers often keep a notebook that's very much like a scrapbook. It's called a **journal**. It's a place for you to keep anything that has to do with writing—words, lists, drawings, even doodles. Many writers get their best writing ideas from their journals.

November 29

We went to Grandmother's house for Thanksgiving dinner yesterday. Grandmother let me carry the turkey from the kitchen to the table. Suddenly the turkey slipped and fell off the plate. Aunt Jane made a wild dive and caught it just before it hit the floor. Boy, was I embarrassed! Thinking about it now, though, I guess it was pretty funny.

Maybe I'll write a story about it.

Talk About the Model

★ Why did the writer write about this experience in her journal?

★ Which sentences tell you how she felt?

★ Why do you think this experience would make a good story?

Start your own journal. Use a notebook with plenty of space to write.

- Start each entry with the date.

- Write about something you want to remember. You can make notes or lists or write whole sentences.

- Make doodles or drawings if you want to.

- Add photos, pictures, or other things you want to save.

- Choose a quiet time and write in your journal every day.

Writer's Tip
You can find lots of writing ideas in your journal. Look for events that you remember clearly.

Writing Paragraphs

A group of sentences about one subject or idea is a **paragraph.** Put together several paragraphs about a subject and you have a piece of writing, such as a story, a letter, or a book report.

A paragraph is made up of a topic sentence and detail, or supporting, sentences. The **topic sentence** tells the main idea of the paragraph. It's often the first sentence of the paragraph. **Detail sentences** add facts and information about the main idea.

Meet the Writer

The topic sentence tells the main idea. Once I write that, the details are easy to add. I wrote about the time my dad took me on a roller coaster.

Jessinia Dwight
North Carolina

The first time I went on a roller coaster, I was excited and scared at the same time. My heart was pounding as my dad and I climbed into the little car. The car started to move. Slowly we climbed up and up. All I could see was the blue sky above me. Suddenly we dropped down. I closed my eyes as we started to go faster. My stomach did a flip, and I held on as tight as I could. I felt the wind against my face. It was great!

Talk About the Model

★ Which sentence tells the main idea of the paragraph?

★ Which sentences give you more information about the main idea?

★ What would be a good title for this paragraph?

Your Turn

Write your own paragraph. Think of a subject you know a lot about.

- Write a topic sentence. Indent the first word.
- Add some sentences that give facts and details about your topic.
- You may want to end your paragraph with a sentence that sums up your information.

Conferencing

Read your paragraph to a partner. Have your partner identify the main idea. Ask whether you've given enough information about your main idea.

Tech Tip
Remember to name your file and to save it when you finish.

Writer's Tip
Every paragraph needs a topic sentence and information that tells about the topic.

Writing Summaries

Have you ever looked at the TV listings in the newspaper? These listings tell you what a program is about. They sum up a whole program in just one or two sentences.

A **summary** can also help you remember what you've read. It tells the most important ideas in one or two sentences. Michael wrote a summary from *Digging Dinosaurs* by Judy Nayer.

Meet the Writer

First, I decide what facts I want to remember. Then, I put the ideas into my own words. I wrote this summary from a book about dinosaurs.

Michael Simone
Michigan

from *Digging Dinosaurs*
by Judy Nayer

For nearly 180 million years, the dinosaurs ruled the earth. Then, about 65 million years ago, they all disappeared.

Many scientists think that comets hit the earth 65 million years ago. Comets are huge balls of ice and rock that travel through space. If comets really did hit the earth, clouds of dust would have blown up into the air. These dust clouds would have blocked the sun's light. No plants could have grown. Plant-eating dinosaurs would have died because there was no food. Without plant eaters for food, the meat eaters would have died, too.

<u>Digging Dinosaurs</u>   page 42

   Dinosaurs lived on the earth for a long time and then disappeared. Many scientists think comets hit the earth. Clouds of dust from the comets blocked out the sun. Without plants for food, the dinosaurs all died.

                                        Summary

Talk About the Model

★ What information did the writer want to remember?

★ Why did the writer put the information in his own words?

Choose a page from your science or social studies book and write a summary of it.

- Read the page carefully.
- Remember, a summary tells only the most important information or the main ideas. Look for main ideas in the title and in the first and last sentences or paragraphs.
- Write the summary in your own words.

Making Organizers, Charts, and Graphs

Meet the Writer

I use diagrams to help me organize my writing. Sometimes I also use charts and graphs to explain something to the reader.

Angela Foster
Arizona

Writing needs organization. That's why **organizers, charts,** and **graphs** can be helpful. They can present information more clearly than words alone can.

Organizers

Writers use **organizers** to help them plan what they are going to write. There are different organizers for different kinds of writing. Here are two diagrams that are used as organizers.

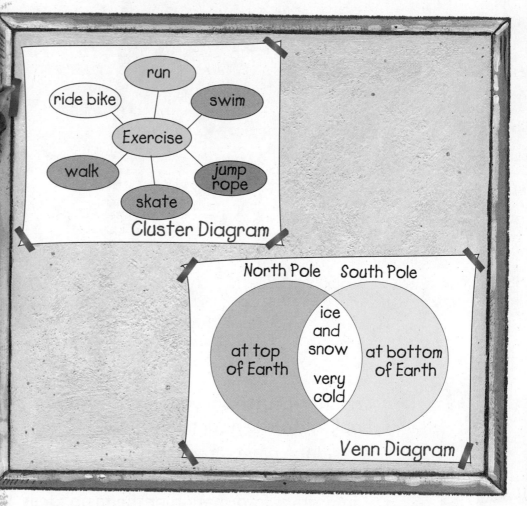

run

ride bike

swim

Exercise

walk

jump rope

skate

Cluster Diagram

North Pole   South Pole

at top of Earth

ice and snow

very cold

at bottom of Earth

Venn Diagram

Talk About the Models

★ What kind of writing would a cluster diagram help you plan?

★ Why is a Venn diagram a good way to compare two things?

Charts

Charts are another way to organize your writing. They can help you stick to the topic and keep your ideas in order.

1. I go fishing with my uncle.

2. We find a good place and throw our lines into the water.

3. I catch a big fish. My uncle catches a tiny fish.

4. "Maybe I should teach you," I say, and we go home.

Story Chart

Inventions

I. Inventions that changed our lives

A. Edison's electric light

B. Goddard's rocket engine

II. Inventions that save lives

A. Lasers for surgery

B. Antibiotics

Outline

Talk About the Models

★ What does a story chart help you do?

★ What kind of writing could you use an outline for?

Graphs

Writers often use **graphs** when they talk about numbers of things and how to compare them. The bar graph below shows how many students are in each grade.

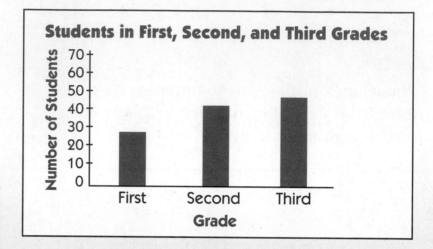

Students in First, Second, and Third Grades

Talk About the Model

★ Why do graphs work better than words to talk about numbers?

★ In what kinds of writing would you use a graph?

Your Turn

Work alone or in a small group to make your own organizers, charts, and graphs. Follow the directions.

- Plan a report on dolphins. Use a cluster diagram to show facts and details you might include. Start with dolphins as the main idea.

- Make a Venn diagram to compare dolphins and whales.

- Make an outline of main ideas and details.

- Make a bar graph that compares the weights of a dolphin, a whale, a porpoise, and a person. First, find out how much each one weighs.

ONCE UPON A TIME

Writing to Tell a Story

Writing a Narrative Paragraph

Stories are fun to read, especially when they're about real people. In a **narrative paragraph**, the writer tells a story about something that really happened. The events, characters, and setting are real. Often the writer is the main character.

Meet the Writer

I often go to baseball games with my family. At one game, my sister Jenny did something so unbelievable I had to write about it.

Josh Stein
Illinois

A Great Catch
by Josh Stein

Last Friday, my family and I went to a baseball game. It was the last inning. No one had hit a ball anywhere near us the whole game. Dad let Jenny hold his baseball glove. Jenny doesn't even play baseball! Suddenly, Dad dropped his popcorn. Mom stood like a statue. I looked up and saw a baseball heading right at us. Before I knew it, Jenny stuck out Dad's glove. Kaboom! The ball landed right in the mitt. Jenny jumped up and down, screaming, "I caught it!" I'll never forget it.

Talk About the Model

★ How does the writer show that the story really happened to him?

★ How does the writer feel about what Jenny did?

Make a Plan

Write your own narrative paragraph. To organize your ideas, start with a plan. Fold a sheet of paper in half and then in half again. Label the boxes *Who, What, Where,* and *When.* Fill in the four sections with notes that answer these questions.

- Who are the characters? Describe them.
- What happens?
- When and where does the story take place?

Write It Down

- Start your paragraph with a topic sentence that tells *who, when,* and *where.*
- Tell the story. Use words like *first, then,* and *later* to make the order of the story clear.
- Use words that tell how things looked, sounded, smelled, tasted, and felt.

Conferencing

Read your paragraph to a partner. Is there anything you should change to make the story clearer or more interesting?

Look It Over

Read your paragraph out loud. Do the details all tell about the main idea? Do you use complete sentences?

Writer's Tip
If you are handwriting your draft, write on every other line. This will make your work easier to revise.

Portfolio

Save your paragraph. You may want to write more and make it into a longer story.

Writing a Picture Essay

What do you remember when you look at a family photograph? Pictures can bring back good memories. Like words, pictures can tell a story. A **picture essay** uses words and pictures to tell a story.

In *Uncle Phil's Diner,* the author remembers a special time with her father. The words and pictures work together to make the author's memories come alive. This is how the story begins.

Meet the Writer

Helena Clare Pittman wrote *Uncle Phil's Diner* about her family.

Uncle Phil's Diner
BY HELENA CLARE PITTMAN

Writing connects you to your dreams, memories, and the things you never want to forget.

Each picture has two or three sentences that describe it and tell the story.

The wind is singing through the bare maple branches. They tap against my window, bobbing with fresh fallen snow. It's Sunday, and Papa and I are going to Uncle Phil's for breakfast.

The story is told in the first person.

The words add details about what the characters said and did.

The pictures show how the characters look and feel.

I rush down the hall to wake him up, but the big bed is already made. I race downstairs and through the swinging kitchen door.

"Papa, are we going?"

"A little snow won't keep us home. But it's too cold to go in pajamas!" he teases.

I gallop back up the stairs and nearly trip over Muffin, lacing through my legs.

"Two sweaters, Ruthie!" Mama calls from the kitchen.

I hurry to get dressed and put on my galoshes.

Muffin sniffs the cold wind at the door. She's happy to be staying home.

Mama wraps a wool scarf around my neck. "Keep warm!" she says, hugging me. "Send my love to Phil and Ida and the girls!"

At last Papa and I start down the street. The diner is ten blocks away.

The pictures are shown in the order that the events happened.

Talk About the Model

As a Reader

★ How does the author introduce the main character and the setting?

★ How do the pictures and words work together to tell the story?

As a Writer

★ Why did the author make the book look like a photo album?

★ Why did the author write about this experience?

Make a Plan

Decide on a Story

You need two things for a picture essay — ideas and pictures. Start by brainstorming a list of ideas for a story. Is this going to be a true story about you and your family or one you made up? Once you've decided on a topic, you need to fill in the details. Use the following chart to organize your story.

Characters		
Setting (time and place)		
What happens		
Beginning	Middle	End
1.	1.	1.
2.	2.	2.
3.	3.	3.

Who, What, and When?

As you make your chart, answer the following questions.

- Who are the characters?
- When and where does the story take place?
- What happens to the characters?
- How does the story end?

Organize Your Pictures

In a picture essay, the pictures are as important as the words.

- First, draw or paint pictures for each step of the story. Use your chart as a guide.
- Next, arrange the pictures in the order that the events happened.
- Leave enough space near each picture to write two or three sentences.

Write It Down

- Write two or three sentences near each picture.
- Remember to introduce the characters and tell about where and when the story takes place.
- For each picture, tell what is happening in the story and add details that the picture doesn't show.

Tech Tip

If you type your story, leave extra space between each group of sentences. When you finish, cut them apart.

Portfolio

Keep pictures, notes, and drafts in your portfolio. This will help you make changes as you work.

Conferencing

Share your story with a partner or small group. Are the story and pictures clear? Is there any information you need to add?

Look It Over

Read your picture essay again. Did you tell the story in the order the events happened? Are there any details you need to add? Is your handwriting neat and clear?

A Story About Me

Every day you have new adventures and experiences. When you write a story about something that happened to you, it's called a **personal narrative.** You're the star of the story. The events, setting, and characters are all real.

Meet the Writer

I love to shop, especially in big stores. Once, my friends and I got lost. We were really scared. I wrote about it because I'll never forget it.

Miriam Pate
Tennessee

A Personal Narrative

★ Focuses on one experience that happened to the writer

★ Has a beginning that introduces the characters and setting

★ Has a middle that describes a problem or situation

★ Has an end that tells how the problem was solved

★ Is written in the first person

Think It Through

The first step in writing a personal narrative is choosing a topic. Sometimes this can seem like the hardest part. Here are some ideas and activities to get you started.

Brainstorming

A good way to find a topic is to brainstorm a list of things you have done. Then expand this list by adding some details about what happened. This is the chart that Miriam made.

What I Did	What Happened
1. went to the beach	1. built a sand castle
2. shopped with friends	2. got lost
3. jumped rope	3. scraped my knee
4. rode my bike	4. got chased by a dog

Make a chart like Miriam's. List four or five things you have done. Then list specific things that happened to you.

Select a Topic

Read your brainstorming list again.

- Which topic do you like the most? Why?
- Which do you remember the most details about?
- Which do you think other people will enjoy reading about?

Choose one topic and circle it.

Design a Plan

Miriam decided to write about a trip to the store where something unexpected happened to her and her friends. She made a story map to help plan the beginning, middle, and end of her story.

The beginning introduces the subject, characters, and setting.

BEGINNING

What?   went shopping with friends
Who?   me, Kristi, Alex, Mrs. Shirley
Where?   Kidz Stuff, a department
             store for kids

The middle tells what happened.

MIDDLE

• went to restroom with Kristi
• ran through the clothes
• couldn't find Alex and Mrs. Shirley

The end tells how everything turned out.

END

• loudspeaker called our names
• found my friends
• felt happy!

Writer's Tip
You always can change your story map. If you remember more details, just go back and add them.

Create your own story map. These questions will help you decide what to include.

• Who are the characters in your story?
• What happened to you and the other characters?
• How did everything work out?
• How did you feel about what happened?

Conferencing

Share your story map with a partner. What does your partner think of your plan?

Portfolio

Save your prewriting notes. They'll help you make sure you've included all the important information.

Drafting

Put It Into Words

Before she started writing, Miriam tried to remember everything that happened that day. She followed her story map as she wrote. Have you ever had an experience like Miriam's?

My Lost-and-Found Trip
by Miriam Pate

Beginning

One day, I went to Kidz Stuff with Kristi, Alex, and Kristi and Alex's mom, Mrs. Shirley. I never thought a shopping trip could be such an adventure.

Middle

On our way to the restroom, we were going through the racks of clothes as if we were in a jungle. We did not kno that Alex and Mrs. Shirley were following us. When we came out of the restroom, we went back to the toys. That's where Mrs. Shirley and Alex were when we left. The toys were awesome!

End

We couldn't find them. We looked down every aisle. They weren't anywhere.

"hey, the lady on the loudspeaker just called out our names," said Kristi. So we went to the manager, and their they were.

Think Like a Writer

As you write your first draft, ask yourself

★ **Subject:** What experience am I writing about?

★ **Audience:** Whom do I want to read my narrative?

★ **Purpose:** What do I want my readers to get from my story?

★ **Form:** What are the main points of a personal narrative?

Your Turn

Now you're ready to write your first draft. Review your story map. Don't worry about making mistakes or leaving out things. Just write. You can make changes later.

Drafting Checklist

- You are the main character. Use *I* and *me* to tell what *you* did.
- Catch the reader's interest in the first paragraph. Tell who the characters are and what the setting is.
- In the middle part of the story, tell what happens. Use details to help your readers see, hear, and feel what happened.
- In the end, tell how everything works out.
- Give your narrative an interesting title.

Conferencing

Read your first draft to a partner. Does the story have a clear beginning, middle, and end? Is the story written in the first person?

Writer's Tip
You may wish to write your first draft on yellow lined paper and your final copy on white paper.

Tech Tip
When you pick a name for your file, choose one that tells something about the story so you can find it quickly.

Portfolio
Clip your notes together and label them before you put them in your portfolio.

Take Another Look

Miriam read her personal narrative and thought about ways to improve it. She wanted to make it more exciting. She also got advice from her writing partner. How do her changes improve her story?

My Lost-and-Found Trip
by Miriam Pate

Add a sentence to explain the plot more clearly. ⟶

One day, I went to Kidz Stuff with Kristi, Alex, and

Kristi and Alex's mom, Mrs. Shirley. I never thought a

The trouble started when Mrs. Shirley let Kristi and
I go to the restroom by ourselves.

shopping trip could be such an adventure.

Use a word that better describes what they were doing. ⟶

sneaking
On our way to the restroom, we were going through

the racks of clothes as if we were in a jungle. We did not

Add a word to make the meaning of a sentence clear. ⟶

kno that Alex and Mrs. Shirley were following us. When

department
we came out of the restroom, we went back to the toys.

Take out a sentence that has nothing to do with the story. ⟶

That's where Mrs. Shirley and Alex were when we left.

~~The toys were awesome!~~

Add dialogue to tell how the writer feels. ⟶

We couldn't find them. We looked down every aisle. They
"I'm scared," I said.
weren't anywhere.

"hey, the lady on the loudspeaker just called out our

Add a sentence to the end of the story about how the writer felt. ⟶

names," said Kristi. So we went to the manager, and
It felt great to be back together!
their they were.

Read your first draft slowly. What parts do you think are good? Which would you like to change?

Don't worry about marking up your first draft. Make any changes you want. Use the Revising Checklist to help you.

Revising Marks

≡	capitalize
∧	add
✛	remove
⊙	add a period
/	make lowercase
∽	move
∾	transpose

Revising Checklist

- Is the story told in the first person?
- Is there a beginning, middle, and end to the story?
- Does the dialogue make the story more interesting?
- Are there interesting details about the characters and setting?

Conferencing

Work with a partner to answer the Revising Checklist questions. In the margin of your draft, write notes to help you remember if something needs to be added or taken out.

Tech Tip

The Cut and Paste tools of your word-processing program will help you move words, sentences, or even whole paragraphs.

Portfolio

Save your revisions and drafts in your portfolio until you are ready to edit and proofread.

Become a Super Writer

Use dialogue to make your writing more true to life. See the *Writer's Handbook* section, page 211, for help.

Polish Your Writing

Miriam thought her story was good, but she wanted to do the best job she could. She checked her draft and found a few spelling and grammar mistakes to correct. Did she miss any?

My Lost-and-Found Trip
by Miriam Pate

Replace two nouns with a pronoun. ......▶

One day, I went to Kidz Stuff with Kristi, Alex, and ~~Kristi~~
their
~~and Alex's~~ mom, Mrs. Shirley. I never thought a shopping trip

could be such an adventure. The trouble started when

Replace an incorrect pronoun. ....▶

me
Mrs. Shirley let Kristi and I go to the restroom by ourselves.

Correct the spelling of a word with the long o sound. ....▶

On our way to the restroom, we were sneaking through

know
the racks of clothes as if we were in a jungle. We did not (kno)

that Alex and Mrs. Shirley were following us. When we came

out of the restroom, we went back to the toy department.

That's where Mrs. Shirley and Alex were when we left.

We couldn't find them. We looked down every aisle. They

weren't anywhere. "I'm scared," I said.

Capitalize the first letter of a quotation. ....▶

"hey, the lady on the loudspeaker just called out our

Correct the spelling of an easily confused word. ....▶

there
names," said Kristi. So we went to the manager, and ~~their~~ they

were. It felt great to be back together!

Read your paper slowly and carefully, just as Miriam did. Check for grammar, spelling, and punctuation. Use the Editing and Proofreading Checklist for help.

Proofreading Marks

¶	indent first line of paragraph
≡	capitalize
∧ or ∨	add
✄	remove
⊙	add a period
/	make lowercase
○	spelling mistake
⊃	move
∼	transpose

Editing and Proofreading Checklist

- Did I spell all words correctly?
  See pages 262–271 in the *Writer's Handbook* section.
- Did I use personal pronouns, such as *I*, *me*, and *my*, correctly in sentences?
  See page 245 in the *Writer's Handbook* section.
- Did I use capital letters in quotations and at the beginning of sentences?
  See pages 248 and 252 in the *Writer's Handbook* section.
- Did I write in complete sentences?
  See page 227 in the *Writer's Handbook* section.

Conferencing

Share your story with a partner. Ask if you used personal pronouns correctly.

Writer's Tip
Use a dictionary to check the spelling of a word.

Portfolio

Clip everything together and store it in your folder until you are ready to publish it.

Become a Super Writer

Remember to use simple and complex sentences that have a subject and a predicate. See pages 226–227 in the *Writer's Handbook* section.

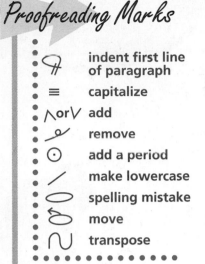

Share Your Work

The story made Miriam remember how scared she was that day. She was glad everything had worked out. Miriam made her final copy and then decided to illustrate it. What part of the story would make a good picture?

My Lost-and-Found Trip
by Miriam Pate

One day, I went to Kidz Stuff with Kristi, Alex, and their mom, Mrs. Shirley. I never thought a shopping trip could be such an adventure. The trouble started when Mrs. Shirley let Kristi and me go to the restroom by ourselves.

On our way to the restroom, we were sneaking through the racks of clothes as if we were in a jungle. We did not know that Alex and Mrs. Shirley were following us. When we came out of the restroom, we went back to the toy department. That's where Mrs. Shirley and Alex were when we left.

We couldn't find them. We looked down every aisle. They weren't anywhere. "I'm scared," I said.

"Hey, the lady on the loudspeaker just called out our names," said Kristi. So we went to the manager, and there they were. It felt great to be back together!

Now it's time to let readers enjoy your work. Here are some ideas for sharing personal narratives in your class or at home.

Writer's Gallery ▶

Display your personal narrative. Place your work on a wall or on a stand at your desk so others can enjoy it. You may want to make a cover for your story or paint a picture about it.

◀ Story Time

In small groups, you and your classmates can take turns reading your personal narratives aloud to each other. Your group can decide if there should be a question-and-answer period after each narrative is read.

Act It Out ▶

Act out your personal narrative. Ask classmates to play the different characters in your story. Remind each character to speak clearly.

Writing Riddles

Here's your chance to have some fun with words. A **riddle** describes an object but doesn't name it. You have to use the clues to guess the answer. Do you have a favorite riddle?

Meet the Writer

I love riddles. My friends and I take turns making them up for each other. I wrote these just for you.

Brenda Rivera
New York

1. I can be worn on a wrist or hung on a wall. I don't speak, but I tell something. What am I?

A riddle has one or more sentences that describe an object.

2. What climbs the stairs but doesn't have legs?

The subject of a riddle is an everyday object.

3. What can you catch but never throw?

A riddle is asked in the form of a question.

Talk About the Models

★ What clues does the writer give to help you guess the answers to the riddles?

★ Which riddles were you able to answer?

4. I'm a room, but I don't have any windows or doors. What am I?

5. What's black and white and read all over?

Descriptive words tell about the object's color, size, shape, sound, and use.

Answers: 1. A watch or clock 2. A carpet
3. A cold 4. A mushroom
5. A newspaper.

Make a Plan

Follow these steps to plan a riddle.

- Choose an object to write about.
- Put the object you choose in the center of a cluster.
- Write things about the object, such as its size, shape, color, and use. Use Brenda's cluster as a model.

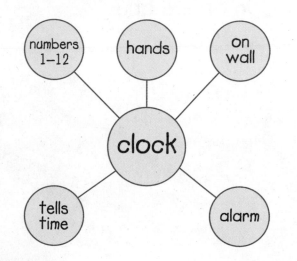

Tech Tip

Illustrate your riddles with clip art or pictures from a graphics or word-processing program.

Write It Down

- Think of one or two clues.
- Use words that tell about the object's size, shape, color, sound, and use.
- Start your sentence with either "What is . . ." or "I am . . ."
- Make your clues funny.

Portfolio

Save all your notes and drafts so you can write more riddles later.

Conferencing

See if your partner can answer your riddles. Do you give enough clues? Are they clear?

Look It Over

Have you used enough details to make your riddles interesting and fun? Did you end your question with a question mark?

Make It Real!

Some stories seem so real that we believe they could actually happen. These stories are called **realistic stories.** Everything in a realistic story is made up, but everything in it could really happen.

A Realistic Story

★ Uses a real event as a starting point

★ Has a beginning that introduces the characters and setting

★ Has a middle that describes a problem or situation

★ Has an end that tells how the problem was solved

★ Tells events in order

Meet the Writer

I like camping with my friends. One night, something strange happened in the woods. It gave me a good idea for a story.

Shane Smith
Virginia

Has anything exciting happened to you that might make a good realistic story? Remember, you can start with a real experience and then change any detail to make it more interesting.

Brainstorming

Shane read through his journal and came up with several ideas for a story. He decided to write about a camping trip. Shane made a chart that showed two kinds of things—what actually happened on the camping trip and what could have happened.

What Happened?

1. roasted marshmallows
2. caught some fish
3. went on a hike

What Could Have Happened?

1. scared by animals
2. caught in a flood
3. lost in the woods at night

Your Turn

What have you done that might make a good realistic story? To get ideas, read your journal or talk to your family and friends. When you have some ideas, make a chart like Shane's to see which one might make the best story.

Select a Topic

Choose the topic you like best. Ask yourself the following questions.

- Are the characters and the setting realistic?
- Is the situation or problem in the story believable?
- How do the characters work out their problem?

Design a Plan

When you tell a story, it's a good idea to think about your story's problem and how the characters solve it. Shane used a special story map to help him plan his realistic story.

Beginning	Middle	End
Four boys go camping in the woods	1. Sleep in tents 2. Cook hot dogs around the campfire 3. Hear a scary noise 4. Think it's wolves	1. Mice made the noise 2. Boys think it's funny

Now it's time for you to create your own story map. Follow Shane's plan. Think about what you will include in the beginning, middle, and end. These questions will help you.

- When and where does the story take place?
- Who are your characters?
- What happens to them?
- How is the problem solved?

Conferencing

Talk about your story map with a partner. Ask if the story could have really happened. Should anything be added or taken out?

Portfolio

You will need your plan and notes later, so save them in your portfolio.

Put It Into Words

Shane followed his story map when he wrote his first draft. He wanted to get his story down on paper as fast as he could. He also wanted to surprise readers with his ending. Were you surprised?

The Camping Trip
by Shane Smith

The beginning introduces the characters and setting.

One day, there were four boys named Josh, Jack, Danny, and Alex. Joshs dad took them camping over the weekend. Jack and Danny had never been camping before.

When they got to the campsite, it was almost dark First, they started a fire and cooked some hot dogs. Then, everybody got in their sleeping bags around the fire. All of a sudden,

The middle tells about a problem.

they heard a noise. It was very scary. "What was that?" Jack whispered.

Then they saw little glowing eyes in the darkness. The

The end shows how the problem is solved.

glowing eyes came closer and closer but when they got near the fire, what do you think they were. The glowing eyes were three little mice. Everybody started to laugh.

Think Like a Writer

Here are some things to think about when you write your first draft.

★ **Subject:** What is the main event?

★ **Audience:** Who will read my story?

★ **Purpose:** How can I make my story interesting?

★ **Form:** What are the main features of a realistic story?

Your Turn

Now it's time to write your own realistic story. Follow your story map. If you run out of ideas or get stuck, simply stop and write any words that come to mind about the scene you are creating. That should get you back on track again. Use the Drafting Checklist to guide you.

Drafting Checklist

- Start your story with a real event.
- Write about a problem that could really happen.
- Tell events in the order in which they happen.
- Be sure your story has a clear beginning, middle, and end.

Conferencing

Read your first draft to your partner. Ask if the problem is clear. What does your partner think about the ending? Could the story have really happened?

Take Another Look

Shane was pleased with the way his story was shaping up. To make it even better, though, he would have to make some changes. How do you think these changes improved his story?

Add a better title to catch reader's attention. •••••••••••➤

The Very Scary Sound
~~The Camping Trip~~
by Shane Smith

Delete unimportant information. ••••➤ ~~One day, there were four boys named~~ Josh, Jack, Danny,

Add a detail to make writing more interesting. •••➤ were good friends

and Alex. Joshs dad took them camping over the weekend.

Jack and Danny had never been camping before.

When they got to the campsite, it was almost dark First, they

started a fire and cooked some hot dogs. Then, everybody

Add words that describe what the noise sounds like. •••➤ got in their sleeping bags around the fire. All of a sudden,
                              crunch, crunch, crunch.
they heard a ~~noise.~~ It was very scary.

Add humor to keep the reader's interest. ••➤

"What was that?" Jack whispered.

"Its a pack of wolves coming to eat us!" Alex said. Danny got up to leave.

Replace an overused adjective. •••➤
Then they saw little glowing eyes in the darkness. The
        yellow
~~glowing~~ eyes came closer and closer but when they got near

the fire, what do you think they were. The glowing eyes were

three little mice. Everybody started to laugh.

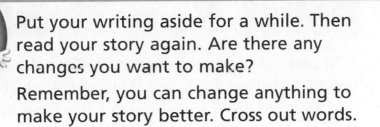

Put your writing aside for a while. Then read your story again. Are there any changes you want to make?

Remember, you can change anything to make your story better. Cross out words. Cut the paper into sections and glue the sections back in a different order. Use the Revising Checklist as a guide.

Revising Marks

≡	capitalize
∧	add
ℓ	remove
⊙	add a period
/	make lowercase
◠	move
∾	transpose

Revising Checklist

- Is the story believable?
- Is there a problem? Is it solved?
- Does the story have a beginning, a middle, and an end?
- Are there interesting details about the characters and the setting?
- Does the dialogue make the story more interesting?

Tech Tip
Save the different drafts of your story. Ask your teacher how to name each one.

Conferencing

Get together with a partner or small group and read your story. Does the story keep your partner's interest?

Portfolio

Clip your revisions together in your portfolio until you are ready to edit and proofread your writing.

Become a Super Writer

As you write, think about what you would say if you were telling the story to a group of friends. For help with voice, see the *Writer's Handbook* section, page 223.

Polish Your Writing

Shane felt he was almost done. Once he fixed a few small mistakes, he would be finished. He used proofreading marks to show the errors he found. Do you think he found everything?

Add an apostrophe to show that something belongs to someone.

Indent the first word of a paragraph and put a period at the end of a sentence.

Add an apostrophe in a contraction.

Split a run-on sentence into two sentences.

Replace a period with a question mark at the end of a question.

The Very Scary Sound
by Shane Smith

Josh, Jack, Danny, and Alex were good friends. Joshs dad took them camping over the weekend. Jack and Danny had never been camping before.

¶ When they got to the campsite, it was almost dark First, they started a fire and cooked some hot dogs. Then, everybody got in their sleeping bags around the fire. All of a sudden, they heard a crunch, crunch, crunch. It was very scary.

"What was that?" Jack whispered.

"Its a pack of wolves coming to eat us!" Alex said. Danny got up to leave. Then they saw little glowing eyes in the darkness. The yellow eyes came closer and closer but when they got near the fire, what do you think they were. The glowing eyes were three little mice. Everybody started to laugh.

Now it's time to give your story a final check. Read it carefully. Did you use commas and periods correctly? Are all words spelled correctly? Use the Editing and Proofreading Checklist as a guide.

⊄	indent first line of paragraph
≡	capitalize
∧ or ∨	add
⤸	remove
⊙	add a period
/	make lowercase
◯	spelling mistake
⤴	move
∩	transpose

Editing and Proofreading Checklist

- Did I check for run-on sentences?
  See page 229 in the *Writer's Handbook* section.
- Did I use apostrophes correctly in contractions and with possessive nouns?
  See page 259 in the *Writer's Handbook* section.
- Did I indent the first word of a paragraph and place a period at the end of a sentence?
  See page 253 in the *Writer's Handbook* section.

Tech Tip
The Spelling tool doesn't catch all spelling mistakes. Proofread your work carefully.

Conferencing

Show your story to a partner. Ask if you used quotation marks correctly to show what someone said?

Portfolio
Put your notes, drafts, and computer disks in your portfolio until you are ready to publish your story.

Become a Super Writer

Remember to indent new paragraphs and to give each sentence the correct end mark. For help, see the *Writer's Handbook* section, pages 253 and 255.

Share Your Work

After Shane wrote his final copy, he drew a picture to illustrate his story. He planned to display his story in the classroom.

The Very Scary Sound
by Shane Smith

Josh, Jack, Danny, and Alex were good friends. Josh's dad took them camping over the weekend. Jack and Danny had never been camping before.

When they got to the campsite, it was almost dark. First, they started a fire and cooked some hot dogs. Then, everybody got in their sleeping bags around the fire. All of a sudden, they heard a crunch, crunch, crunch. It was very scary.
"What was that?" Jack whispered.

"It's a pack of wolves coming to eat us!" Alex said. Danny got up to leave. Then they saw little glowing eyes in the darkness. The yellow eyes came closer and closer. When they got near the fire, what do you think they were? The glowing eyes were three little mice. Everybody started to laugh.

Your hard work has paid off. You're done! Here are a few ideas for publishing your story.

Display Your Story ▶

After you make your final copy, you can display your story in the classroom. Ask your teacher to set aside a special place for you and your classmates to post your stories.

◀ Illustrate Your Story

Create an exciting cover for your realistic story and illustrate some parts of it. If you're using a computer, check its graphics programs for clip art. Maybe you could find a good picture to use.

Tell Your Story ▶

Realistic stories are fun to read to classmates, friends, and family members. Stories can be read during Story Hour. While you tell your story, have one or two classmates pantomime what is happening in the story.

Writing a Fantasy Story

In a **fantasy story,** everything is make-believe. The characters, setting, and events all come from the writer's imagination. In "The Secret Word," Phil invents a magic treehouse, a wicked wizard, and a talking dog.

Meet the Writer

Anything can happen in make-believe stories. I let my imagination go and start to write. My dog, Buddy, gave me the idea for this story.

Phil Cooper
California

The Secret Word
by Phil Cooper

Jack was sleeping. He was tired from studying his word list. His mom woke him up. "Jack, I can't find Buddy!"◄········

Jack ran to his Magic Treehouse to look for Buddy. Buddy was his furry little dog. Jack said some magic words. The treehouse spun faster and faster. It landed in the Weird ◄········ World of Words. The houses were funny. They looked like big H's. The streets were shaped like S's. ◄·················

Jack found Buddy in a cage. "How do I get him out?" Jack asked himself. Suddenly, the Wizard of Words came out. He wore a long pointed hat. He had words all over him. "You can't get Buddy out. You need the secret word! Ha-ha. I'll be back with a cage for you!"

Then Buddy spoke, "Quick, get me out. The magic word is KEY!" Jack screamed the ◄········ word, and Buddy was free. When the wizard came back, Jack and Buddy were gone.

Talk About the Model

★ What is real and what is make-believe in the story?

★ How does the writer make the story believable?

★ What do you think of the way the writer ends the story?

A believable problem is introduced.

When two or more words begin with the same sound, it is called *alliteration*.

The setting and characters are make-believe.

The characters solve the problem.

Make a Plan

Choose the Characters, Setting, and Event

Phil made a chart to help him organize his writing. It answers the questions *who*, *where*, *when*, *what*, and *how*. Make a chart like Phil's to plan your own story.

<u>Who</u> are your characters?		
<u>Where</u> does the story take place?		
<u>When</u> does the story take place?		
<u>What</u> problem does the main character face?		
<u>How</u> is the problem solved?		

Put Your Story in Order

A time line is a good way to keep events in order when you plan and write your story. Here's the time line Phil made.

Beginning   **Middle**   **End**

Jack can't find his dog.   He goes to the Weird World of Words.   Jack and dog escape.

Now make a time line for your story. Put the main events in order.

KEY!

Write It Down

Catch the Reader's Attention

- Start off with a question or statement that makes the reader want to know more. Phil used the sentence, "Jack, I can't find Buddy." The reader wants to know who Buddy is and what happened to him.
- Introduce the characters and the setting.

What Happens Next?

- Next, tell about the problem.
- Tell the story in the order that events happened.
- Use dialogue and details to make the characters seem real.

Solve the Problem

- At the end, tell how the characters solved the problem and what happened to them.

Conferencing

Read your first draft to a partner. How did he or she like your story? Take notes and think about your partner's suggestions.

Look It Over

Read your story again. Will the beginning of your story catch the reader's attention? Did you capitalize the names of people and places and the title of your story?

Tech Tip

Choose an interesting typeface when you print your story. Pick a very fancy one for the title.

Portfolio

File your draft with your notes and other drafts. If you decide to publish your story, you may want to revise it.

Writing a Fable

Sometimes a small story can teach a big lesson about life. A **fable** is a short, often funny story that uses animals to teach a moral, or lesson.

Aesop, a Greek author, wrote fables in which the animals talked and acted like people. In the story "The Fox and the Crow," the clever fox easily outsmarts the silly crow.

Meet the Writer

Aesop was an ancient Greek author, who lived from about 620 to 560 B.C. His stories, which are more than 2,500 years old, are still the most popular fables in the world.

THE BEST of AESOP'S FABLES

Talk About the Model

As a Reader

★ How did the fox get the crow to drop the cheese?

★ How do you think the crow felt at the end of the story?

As a Writer

★ Why did the writer choose a crow and a fox as his main characters?

★ What do you think the writer did before he started to write the story?

The Fox and the Crow

by Aesop

One day a crow snatched a piece of cheese from an open cottage window and flew up into a tree, where she sat on a branch to eat it. A fox, walking by, saw the crow and at once wanted the cheese for himself.

"O Crow," he said, "how beautiful your feathers are! And what bright eyes you have! Your wings shine like polished ebony, and your head sparkles like a glistening jewel. If your voice is as sweet as your looks are fair, you must be the queen of birds." The unwary crow believed every word, and to show how sweet her voice was, she opened her mouth to sing. Out dropped the cheese, which the fox instantly gobbled up.

"You may have a voice," he said to the crow as he went on his way, "but whatever happened to your brain?"

First, the setting is introduced.

Then, a problem is created.

The writer uses comparisons with the word *like* to describe the crow.

The main characters are animals that act like people.

The problem is solved.

The story ends with a moral, or lesson.

Make a Plan

Work Backward—Choose a Moral First

In "The Fox and the Crow," the crow listened to the nice things the fox said about her and forgot about the cheese in her beak. She opened her beak to show off her voice—and what happened? The moral is, "Don't believe everything someone tells you."

Make a list of some lessons you might like to write about. Here are some examples from Aesop's fables.

> If you do something quickly to save time, you may have to do it over again.
>
> If you lie, people may not believe you when you do tell the truth.
>
> Don't be greedy or you might lose everything.

Decide on Your Characters and Setting

- First, choose animals or birds to be your characters. Try to use animals that act like people. Here are some examples.

> turtle—slow, patient
> lion—strong, brave
> fox—clever, fast

- Next, decide where your story will take place. Often the setting of a fable is the place where the animals in the story live, like the woods, a pond, or a farm.

Write It Down

Set Up Your Story

- First, introduce the characters, setting, and the problem.
- Include details about how the characters look, sound, act, and talk.

What Happens Next?

- Next, explain the problem and tell what each character did.
- Use dialogue to show what the characters thought and felt.

Tell the Moral at the End

- Explain how the problem was solved. What happened to each character?
- Write down the lesson you want the reader to learn from your story.

Conferencing

Read your fable to a partner. Does your partner understand your moral? Is there anything the animals should do or say to make it clearer?

Tech Tip

Print enough copies for your friends, classmates, and family members.

Writer's Tip

Try reading the animals' words aloud as you write. It will help you make the dialogue realistic.

Look It Over

Read your fable again. Did you use enough descriptive words to tell your story? Did you use commas correctly?

Share Your Work

Fables are great to share. They're short, funny, and can be enjoyed by people of every age. They can be published in many ways.

Story Time

Illustrate and display your fables or bind several fables together in a book. Read your fables aloud to a younger group of children or to your family.

Puppet Show Time

You can act out your fable with shadow puppets. Here are five easy steps to follow.

- On black construction paper, draw and then cut out the shapes of your animals. Attach them to sticks.

- Use a white cloth or white window shade as your shadow screen.

- Place a single 150-watt white light on a table about six feet behind the screen.

- Turn off the classroom lights. Move the puppets around on the screen as the story is read aloud.

Portfolio

File your drafts and revisions as well as your published story.

IMAGINE THAT

Writing to Describe

Writing a Descriptive Paragraph

In a **descriptive paragraph** the writer uses words to create a picture for the reader. The words tell how something feels, looks, sounds, smells, and tastes. In "Flying" the writer describes her new skates.

Meet the Writer

I was so happy when I got in-line skates for my birthday. I wrote this paragraph about what it felt like to put them on and go.

Stacy Tsang
Minnesota

Flying
by Stacy Tsang

I love zooming down the sidewalk on my in-line skates. Each skate has four bright pink wheels. When I skate, the wheels spin faster and faster. They make a noise like a clock—tick, tick, tick. Sometimes I feel like a rocket speeding down the sidewalk. People and places fly by. I love feeling the wind against my face. Skating makes me feel as if I'm flying through the air. Zoooom! I'm gone.

★ What is the topic sentence?

★ A simile compares two things, using the words *like* or *as*. Find three similes in Stacy's description.

Make a Plan

Think about something you would like to describe. Pick a person, a place, or a thing you know well. Try to make it something or someone that your audience will want to know more about. Then brainstorm a list of describing words that tell about your subject.

subject	look	sound	smell	taste	feel

Write It Down

- Begin with a topic sentence that tells who or what you are describing.
- Give details that tell about your subject. Use the describing words in your list.
- Organize your details so that they make a clear picture of your subject.

Writer's Tip
As you read your paragraph, underline the descriptive words. Make sure that you have enough.

Conferencing

Read your paragraph to a partner or small group. Is there enough detail? Are there any other describing words you could use?

Portfolio

Save your paragraph. You may want to use this description as part of another piece of writing.

Look It Over

Reread your paragraph. Is any detail out of place? Do you have enough describing words to create a picture for your readers?

A **character sketch** describes someone. It tells how they look and act. You can write a character sketch about anyone from your favorite superhero to your Aunt Maude.

A character sketch captures what is most important about a person. This description is from the book *Racing the Sun* by Paul Pitts. In it, young Brandon Rogers meets his Navajo grandfather, who has come from the reservation in Utah to live with him.

Meet the Writer

Paul Pitts lives on a Navajo Reservation where he writes and teaches.

Racing the Sun
Paul Pitts
WINNER OF THE PARENTS' CHOICE AWARD

Writers have to be responsible because what they say has an impact on others.

The writer tells about what he sees, so he writes in the first person, using *I*.

The first sentence introduces the subject of the character sketch.

Grandpa looked the same as the last time I'd seen him —gray-and-white hair worn in a traditional bun at the back of his head, unlined bronze face, earrings made of tiny bone beads with a single turquoise stone, the same straight posture— but somehow he had gotten old.

Talk About the Model

As a Reader

★ What words tell you how Brandon's grandfather looks and acts?

★ How is his grandfather different from the way he was before?

As a Writer

★ How does the writer tell you that his grandfather is old?

★ How does the writer seem to feel about his grandfather? How can you tell?

The blue plaid flannel shirt hung ◄········· loosely from his bony shoulders. The new jeans he wore were cinched so tightly by his old belt with the familiar silver buckle that they ballooned out below the waist. He was moving so ◄·········· slowly and seemed so unsure of himself.

Colorful words tell how the character looks.

Action words tell what the character does.

Make a Plan

Choose a Character

First, you need to choose a person to write about.

- Think of the people you know. Is there someone you really admire?
- Do you have a favorite character from a book? Why do you like that character?

Use the chart below to make a list of people you could write about.

	People I Know	My Favorite Characters
1.		
2.		
3.		

Once you've made your list, ask yourself these questions.

- Who is the most interesting person? Why?
- Whom do I know the most about?
- Can I get more information about this person if I need it?

Collect Facts and Details

Pick one of the people or characters from your list. Make a cluster diagram to organize your details. Use the model to help you.

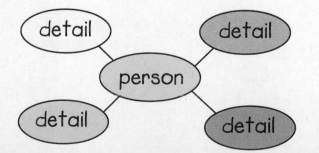

Organize Your Information

Now that you have the facts and details, put them in order. Group together information that tells

- What your subject looks like.
- How your subject acts.
- Why your subject is special. Is your subject an athlete, a superhero, or your best friend?

Write It Down

Review your information before you start to write. What are the most important things you want people to know about your subject?

- In the beginning, identify the person you're writing about.
- Add detail sentences. Describe how the person looks.
- Use action words to tell how the person moves.
- At the end, tell why this person is special.

Conferencing

With a partner, take turns reading each other's character sketches. Ask your partner how well you have shown why the person is special. Ask where you should add more details.

Writer's Tip
Draw a picture or look at a photo of your character. You may see some details you missed.

Tech Tip
Check the Graphics tool on your computer. There may be a border you can use to frame your character sketch.

Look It Over

Read your character sketch again. Do all your words show exactly what this person does and looks like? Prepositional phrases can add interesting details to your writing. Check to see that you used them correctly.

Portfolio

Clip your notes, drafts, and final copy together. Put the final draft on top.

Share Your Work

You can have a lot of fun publishing your character sketch. There are many ways to present it. Here are a few ideas.

Guess Who?

Draw or paint a picture of your character. Make a copy of your character sketch, but take out the character's name. Display your picture and character sketch. Have your classmates guess who your character is. If it is a relative or someone that your classmates don't know, give them some extra hints.

Now Playing...

Write a monologue. A monologue is a speech that a character says alone on stage. You don't have to be an actor to present a monologue of your character sketch. Follow these easy steps.

1. Look over your character sketch to see how the person described can speak, using the words *I* and *me*.

2. Write out your monologue completely and practice saying it aloud with feeling.

3. Add gestures and simple movements that are described in the character sketch.

A Time and a Place

The **setting** is when and where a story takes place. It's important because it often sets the feeling, or mood, for the rest of the story. When you write a description of a setting, use words that make your readers feel as if they are actually there.

A Description of a Setting

★ **Starts with a topic sentence that names the place and time**

★ **Describes the important sights, sounds, and smells and gives other details about the place**

★ **Uses colorful descriptive words to paint a picture for the reader**

Meet the Writer

The park on a sunny day is my favorite place to be. I described it in a story I wrote about my dad teaching me to swing.

DavReen Reed
Virginia

Think It Through

You're not going to write a whole story. You're just going to write a paragraph that describes the setting for a story you might write someday. Make the setting come alive so that readers will wish you had already written the whole story!

Brainstorming

You can start with a place that you like and know well. You can also start with the feeling, or mood, you want for your story.

Check your Observation Log. Is there a place that you've written about in your log that you'd like to describe?

- Start with your log.
- Make a list of different places.
- Write down words that tell how these places make you feel.
- Add words that describe how they look, sound, and smell.

Your Turn

DavReen's List

park	happy bright sun wind in my face
basement	scary smelly dark and dusty
zoo	fun popcorn smell

Select a Topic

Look at your list of setting ideas.
- Which setting do you like the best?
- Which setting can you tell about in detail?
- Which setting leads to a story?

Choose the setting you are going to describe.

Design a Plan

DavReen decided to write about the park. She wanted to create the happy mood she had the day her dad taught her to use the swings. She made a cluster diagram of all the details that described the park.

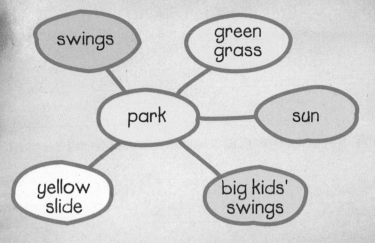

Then she did a quick write about everything she remembered from that day. She wrote quickly to get all her thoughts on paper. She didn't stop until she had run out of things to say.

Your Turn

In the center of a sheet of paper, write the name of the place you want to write about. Then make spokes for all the details and feelings you might include.

Next, do a quick write about the setting you've chosen to describe. Write down everything you remember. Close your eyes and think about how it looked, sounded, and felt. Use your quick write when you write your draft.

Conferencing

Share your plan with a partner. Ask if your partner can picture the setting. Which details help create the mood, or feeling, of the setting? Do you need to add any more details?

Portfolio

Save all your notes and diagrams in your portfolio.

Description Drafting

Put It Into Words

DavReen thought again about the park and the mood she wanted to create. Then she took out her notes and started to write. She tried to picture the scene in her mind as she wrote.

The topic sentence tells the place and time.

The writer uses descriptive words to tell how things looked and felt.

Things are described in the order the writer sees them.

The Park
by DavReen Reed

The park is my favorite place to be early in the morning.

The sun made the park very beautiful. I can feel

the wind blowing as we walk in the gate. The green,

helthy grass flows the way the wind does. Next to the

fence is a yellow slide. The slide is slippery because of

the wind pushing leaves down it. The big kids swings

are moveing in the wind. In the park, everthing is

calm and quiet.

As you write your first draft, ask yourself

★ **Subject:** Have I told the setting and time?

★ **Audience:** Who will read my description?

★ **Purpose:** What do I want my readers to see and feel?

★ **Form:** What do I need to include in a description of a setting?

Start to write the first draft of your description of a setting. As you write, try to picture the place in your mind. If you get stuck and can't think of what to write next, look at your quick write. Use the Drafting Checklist as a guide.

Drafting Checklist

- Write a topic sentence that tells the place and time of your description.
- Include precise, vivid words in your description that clearly express your ideas.
- Make sure all your details tell about the topic.

When you're finished, brainstorm a title for your description.

Conferencing

Share your first draft with a partner. Ask if your partner has ever been to the place you described. What part of your description does your partner like best? Take notes as you listen.

Writer's Tip
A thesaurus can help you find exactly the right word to describe something.

Tech Tip
Practice using the cursor on your computer so that you can easily insert a letter or word where you need it.

Portfolio

If you have made a drawing of your setting, store it in your portfolio along with your first draft.

Take Another Look

DavReen reread her description. She wanted to make sure that her readers could see the park as she pictured it in her head. How did she change her description?

The Park
by DavReen Reed

The park is my favorite place to be early in the morning.

Add a word that describes the park. → warm and
The sun made the park very beautiful. I can feel

the wind blowing as we walk in the gate. The green,

helthy grass flows the way the wind does. Next to the

Replace the word *pushing* with a more accurate word. → fence is a yellow slide. The slide is slippery because of

blowing
the wind ~~pushing~~ leaves down it. The big kids swings

Add a word that describes how the swings are moving. → gently
are moveing in the wind. In the park, everthing is

calm and quiet.

Read your description to yourself more than once. What do you like about it? Could it be the setting of a story? How can you make it better?

Put all your thoughts and changes right on your draft. Now is the time to move sentences around, delete words, and add more description. Use the Revising Checklist to help you decide what changes to make.

Revising Marks

≡	capitalize
∧	add
✔	remove
⊙	add a period
/	make lowercase
◯	move
∼	transpose

Revising Checklist

- Does my topic sentence identify the time and place?
- Are the details of my setting described in some kind of order?
- Does it include words that tell how things feel, look, sound, and smell?

Conferencing

Ask a partner to read your paragraph. Answer the Revising Checklist questions together. Can you and your partner think of other words to add that will bring the setting to life? Are there any words that should come out?

Tech Tip

Remember, don't press the Return key at the end of a line. Let the computer do the work for you.

Portfolio

If you revise your draft more than once, label each one in a different color and keep every version in your portfolio.

Become a Super Writer

To make your writing more interesting, use sensory details. For help, see page 210 in the *Writer's Handbook* section.

Polish Your Writing

It took several revisions, but DavReen knew she had written a good description of a setting. She also saw a few small corrections that still needed to be made.

The Park
by DavReen Reed

Change the tense of a verb.

The park is my favorite place to be early in the morning.

makes

The sun (made) the park very warm and beautiful. I can

Correct a spelling mistake.

feel the wind blowing as we walk in the gate. The green,

healthy

(helthy) grass flows the way the wind does. Next to the

Add an apostrophe to form a possessive noun.

fence is a yellow slide. The slide is slippery because of

the wind blowing leaves down it. The big kids' swings

Correct a spelling mistake.

moving   everything

are (moveing) gently in the wind. In the park, (everthing)

Correct a spelling mistake.

is calm and quiet.

Carefully edit and proofread your paragraph. The Editing and Proofreading Checklist will help you.

Proofreading Marks

¶	indent first line of paragraph
≡	capitalize
∧ or ∨	add
⸰	remove
⊙	add a period
/	make lowercase
◯	spelling mistake
⟀	move
⟲	transpose

Editing and Proofreading Checklist

- Have I used descriptive words to tell about the setting?

  See page 224 in the *Writer's Handbook* section.

- Did I use apostrophes correctly?

  See page 259 in the *Writer's Handbook* section.

- Have I spelled words correctly?

  See pages 262–271 in the *Writer's Handbook* section.

- Is my handwriting neat and easy to read?

  See page 261 in the *Writer's Handbook* section.

Conferencing

Share your description with a partner or small group. Have you used adjectives and adverbs correctly?

Writer's Tip
Use a dictionary to check the spelling of words you're not sure about.

Portfolio
Check your portfolio. Are all your notes and drafts still in the proper place?

Become a Super Writer

Adjectives make your writing come alive. For help, see page 240 in the *Writer's Handbook* section.

Share Your Work

Here is DavReen's description of the park. She wanted everyone to see what the park looked like, so she made a diorama. Do you recognize the girl in the photograph?

The Park
by DavReen Reed

The park is my favorite place to be early in the morning. The sun makes the park very warm and beautiful. I can feel the wind blowing as we walk in the gate. The green, healthy grass flows the way the wind does. Next to the fence is a yellow slide. The slide is slippery because of the wind blowing leaves down it. The big kids' swings are moving gently in the wind. In the park, everything is calm and quiet.

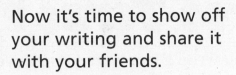

Now it's time to show off your writing and share it with your friends.

Make a Diorama ▶

Make a diorama of your setting. Start with a shoe box. Make the scenery out of cardboard, construction paper, clay, or wood. DavReen even included a photograph of herself!

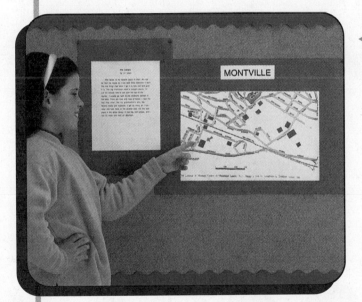

◀ Make a Map

Did any of your classmates write about different places in your community? If they did, mount their descriptions on a map of the town. Use arrows to show the exact places described in the paragraphs.

Music for Your Ears ▶

Listen to tapes of your favorite music. Pick a song or melody that goes well with your setting. Play it on the tape recorder as your classmates read what you wrote.

Writing a Free-Verse Poem

Meet the Writer

In her poetry, Karama Fufuka writes about what it's like to grow up in an urban African-American community.

Karama Fufuka

When you write a **free-verse poem,** you use your imagination to describe something or to tell how you feel. A free-verse poem doesn't have to rhyme, and it doesn't have a particular form. You write it the way you want to.

In the poem "Basketball Star," the author writes about a boy's dream of being the best basketball player in the world. In very few words, she tells a lot about him and how he feels.

My Daddy Is a Cool Dude

Karama Fufuka
pictures by
Mahiri Fufuka

Talk About the Model

As a Reader

★ How does the writer feel about basketball?

★ What pictures form in your mind as you read the poem?

As a Writer

★ Why do you think the writer chose to write in free verse?

★ What do you think the writer wanted the rhythm to remind the reader of?

Basketball Star

by Karama Fufuka

When I get big
I want to be the best
basketball player in the world.
I'll make jump shots, hookballs
and lay-ups
and talk about dribble—
mine'll be outta sight!

The poem has a definite rhythm.

Vivid, exact words name different kinds of basketball shots.

The writer says a lot in very few words.

The writer uses language that matches the feeling of the poem.

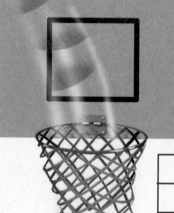

Make a Plan

Are you ready to write your own poem? Remember, poems can be written about any subject. Most poems are written about something that means a lot to the writer. Feelings, thoughts, hopes, dreams, and special moments are all good subjects for free verse.

Collect Your Ideas

- Put yourself in the right mood. Close your eyes. Let ideas come to you.
- Look through your journal for ideas. Think of things you really care about.
- Make a list of things you like to do and experiences that bring back strong feelings and memories.

Things I Like to Do	How It Makes Me Feel
1.	
2.	
3.	

Fill in the Details

- Choose two or three ideas from your list.
- For each one, write as many details as you can think of. Use descriptive words and action words. Your details may be one word or several sentences.
- Read your lists and choose one idea to write your poem about.

Write It Down

Find Your Rhythm

Although free-verse poetry does not rhyme, it does have a rhythm. Rhythm is a pattern made by the sounds of the words. For help with rhythm, see page 220 in the **Writer's Handbook** section.

Tech Tip
Try different typefaces for your poem. Use the Return or Enter key to change line lengths.

Write What You Feel

- Focus on the feelings you want to express.
- Say exactly what you mean to say. Every word counts.
- Don't worry about the form of your poem.

Catch Your Reader's Attention

- Write a first line that catches your reader's attention.
- Use clear, colorful words in every line.
- Choose a good title for your poem.

Conferencing

Read your poem aloud to your partner or to a small group. Ask your partner what words give the best description of your subject. Can your partner tell how you feel about your subject?

Look It Over

Read your poem aloud a few times. How does it sound? Are there any words you should change to make the rhythm smoother and easier to read?

Now look at your poem. How did you break the lines? Are there any lines that are hard to read? Did you use the correct punctuation at the end of each sentence?

Portfolio

Keep all the drafts of your free-verse poem in your portfolio. You may like an earlier draft better.

Share Your Work

Don't feel shy. Poetry should be shared with friends and family. Here are some ways you can publish your poem.

Poetry Reading

Get together with some classmates and have a poetry reading. Take turns reading your poems aloud. Afterward, talk about what you liked about each poem.

Frame Your Work

Your poem is a colorful word picture. Why not make a frame for it? Use construction paper in a bright color to make a frame. Use different things, such as shells, beads, and glitter to decorate your frame. Find a good spot to hang your poem.

Rhyme Time!

Of course, you know what a rhyme is. But in case you forgot, here's a reminder. A rhyme is a pair of words that have the same ending sound, like *go* and *slow* or *fountain* and *mountain*. A **quatrain** is a simple rhyming poem that is only four lines long. It can stand alone or be part of a longer poem.

A quatrain

★ Is a four-line poem in which line 1 rhymes with line 3, and line 2 rhymes with line 4
★ Describes something in an imaginative or unusual way that the writer has seen, thought about, or felt
★ Uses colorful words to describe the subject

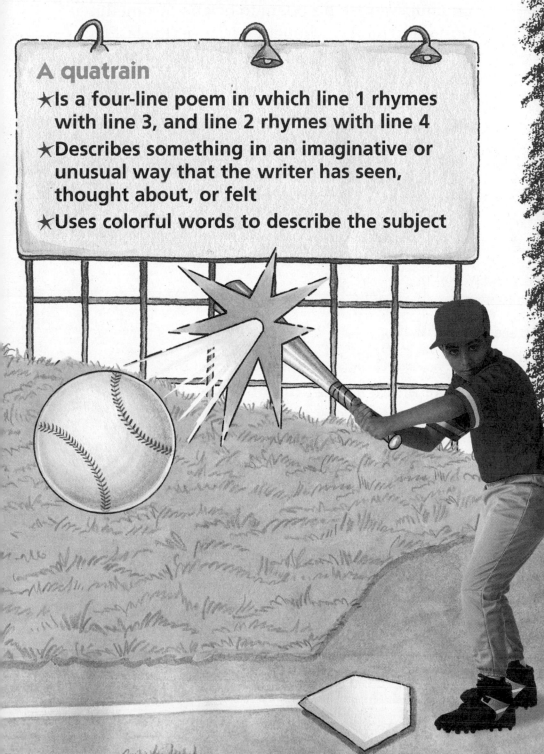

QUATRAIN

Meet the Writer

I wrote about what I love to do most—play baseball. The best feeling in the world is hitting the ball and knowing before you even leave the plate that it's a home run.

Emanuel Campos
Texas

QUATRAIN
Prewriting

Think It Through

What will your poem be about? Get comfortable, close your eyes, and think about what you could describe in four lines. Who will read your poem? Will your poem be just for you, or will you share it?

Brainstorming

Emanuel wanted his poem to be about something important to him. He thought back over the last few months. Then he made an idea sheet and jotted down possible topics.

Emanuel's Idea Sheet

• Finding a bird with a broken wing

• Baseball

• Feeling scared when I got lost

• Going to see my grandfather

Make an idea sheet of your own. List people, places, things, and experiences you could write about. Remember, a poem can be about anything you like.

Select a Topic

Reread your list a few times. Think about each writing idea.

• Which idea do you keep coming back to?

• Which one means the most to you?

• Which one can you remember in the most detail?

Choose the writing idea that will be the most interesting one to work on.

Design a Plan

You've picked a subject for your poem, and now it's time to plan the poem. Remember, the kind of poem you are writing is a quatrain. A quatrain follows a special form.

- Line 1 rhymes with line 3.
- Line 2 rhymes with line 4.

First, Emanuel wrote the word *baseball*, his subject, on a sheet of paper. Then, he wrote a lot of words about his topic, like *bat* and *mitt*. Next, he thought of words that rhymed with each word on his list and added them.

BASEBALL RHYMES

| bat hat | mitt hit | ball wall | base face | score more | cheer hear |

Your Turn

Now make your own list of rhyming words. Write your topic on a sheet of paper. Make a list of words that go with your topic. Add words that rhyme with each word on the list.

When you finish,

- say your rhyming words out loud.
- circle the ones you think might work best.

Conferencing

Share your rhymes with a partner. Ask your partner which rhyming words go best with your topic. Talk about other words that might describe your subject in a colorful way.

Portfolio

Keep your list in your portfolio. Add rhyming words to it as they come to mind during the day.

Drafting

Put It Into Words

Here's the first draft of Emanuel's quatrain. He tried to let his ideas flow, and he tried to make the rhythm of his words sound smooth to his ear. Did he follow the rhyming pattern of a quatrain?

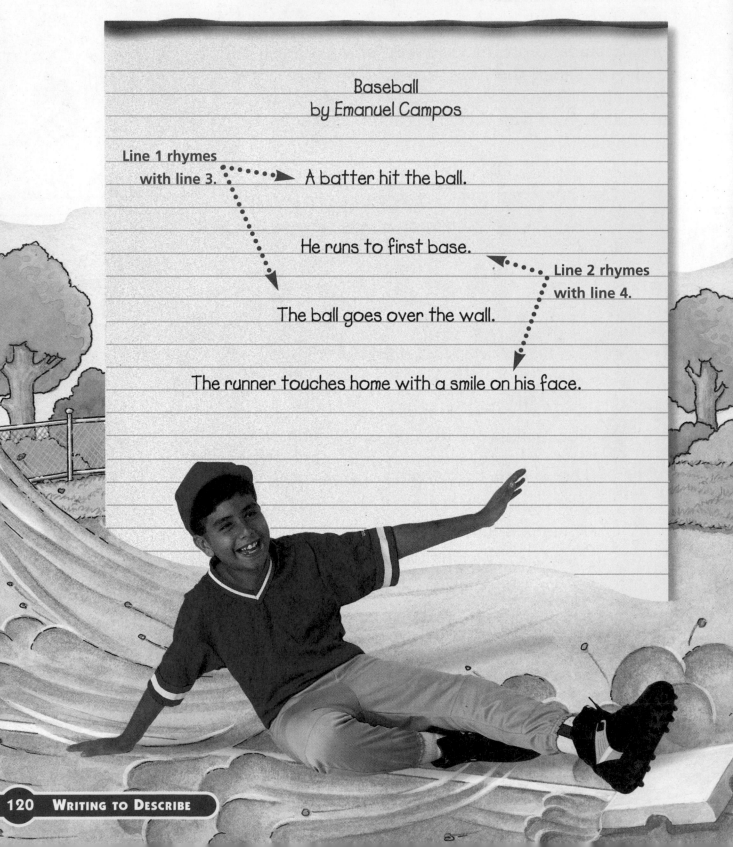

Baseball
by Emanuel Campos

Line 1 rhymes with line 3.

A batter hit the ball.

He runs to first base.

Line 2 rhymes with line 4.

The ball goes over the wall.

The runner touches home with a smile on his face.

As you write your first draft, ask yourself

★ **Subject:** What is my poem about?

★ **Audience:** Who will read my poem?

★ **Purpose:** What do I want to say about baseball?

★ **Form:** What do I need to remember about the form of a quatrain?

Your Turn

Now it's time to write your quatrain. Use your plan to help you. Focus on the person, place, thing, or feeling you want to describe. Look at your list of rhyming words to help give you ideas as you write. You can use the Drafting Checklist as a guide.

Drafting Checklist

• The first line gets the reader's attention.

• Lines 1 and 3 rhyme. Lines 2 and 4 rhyme.

• The poem uses vivid, colorful words that paint a word picture.

• The poem has a rhythm.

• The poem says a lot in a few words.

Tech Tip
Make a backup copy of your poem on a floppy disk. That way you can work on it at home or in school.

Writer's Tip
If you get stuck, put your poem away. Go back and work on it later.

Conferencing

Read your poem out loud to a partner or a small group. Ask if the meaning of your poem is clear. Do the words rhyme? Is there a rhythm to your poem?

Take Another Look

Emanuel's classmates liked the poem, especially the feeling it created. Emanuel still saw some ways to make his poem better. What would you do to improve his poem?

Baseball
by Emanuel Campos

Combine two short sentences into one.

A batter hit the ball. ⸰

and
~~He~~ runs to first base.
∧

The ball goes over the wall.

Shorten the last line to make rhythm better.

See the
~~The runner touches home with~~ a smile on his face.
∧

Now it's your turn to revise your own poem. Read your poem to yourself. How could you make it even better? Make corrections right on your draft. Use this Revising Checklist to help you think about the changes you want to make.

Revising Marks

≡	capitalize
∧	add
℘	remove
⊙	add a period
/	make lowercase
∽	move
∾	transpose

Revising Checklist

- Did you use vivid words to describe your subject?
  See page 224 in the **Writer's Handbook** section.

- Does the first line get the reader's attention?
  See page 219 in the **Writer's Handbook** section.

- Is your poem brief? Should any words be cut?
  See page 221 in the **Writer's Handbook** section.

- Does your poem have the rhythm you want?
  See page 220 in the **Writer's Handbook** section.

Writer's Tip
In poetry, the first word of each new line is usually capitalized.

Portfolio
Save all your drafts as you work. You might want to rethink a change you've made.

Conferencing

Read your poem to a partner. Talk about the questions in the Revising Checklist. Think about any suggestions your partner makes to improve your poem.

Become a Super Writer

The rhythm of a poem makes it read smoothly. For help, see page 220 in the *Writer's Handbook* section.

Polish Your Writing

Emanuel read his revised poem and thought it was much better. But he made a final check to be sure the grammar and spelling were right. He found that he had a few corrections left to make.

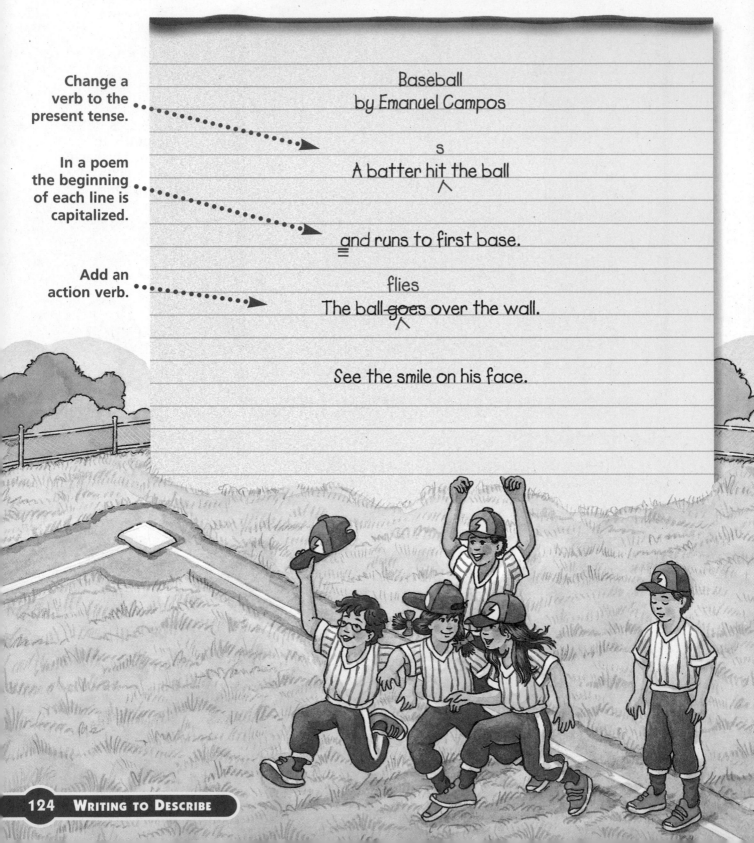

Change a verb to the present tense.

In a poem the beginning of each line is capitalized.

Add an action verb.

Baseball
by Emanuel Campos

s
A batter hit the ball
∧

and runs to first base.

flies
The ball goes over the wall.
∧

See the smile on his face.

Now it's time to polish your quatrain. Read your poem out loud. Keep an eye out for spelling and grammar errors. Use this Editing and Proofreading Checklist to help you.

⊬	indent first line of paragraph
≡	capitalize
∧ or ∨	add
ℓ	remove
⊙	add a period
/	make lowercase
○	spelling mistake
◠	move
ᴎ	transpose

Editing and Proofreading Checklist

- Did I use the correct verb tenses?

  See page 236 in the *Writer's Handbook* section.

- Did I use action verbs to describe what happens?

  See page 234 in the *Writer's Handbook* section.

- Do the subject and verb in each sentence agree?

  See page 237 in the *Writer's Handbook* section.

Conferencing

Share your quatrain with a partner or small group. Are all verbs used correctly? Are there any mistakes?

Tech Tip

Highlight your poem and then click on the Center button to place the poem in the middle of the page.

Portfolio

Put your edited draft on top of your pile of papers. Use it for your final copy.

Become a Super Writer

Action verbs give your reader a better picture of what you are describing. For help with action verbs, see page 234 in the *Writer's Handbook* section.

Share Your Work

Here is Emanuel's finished quatrain. In very few words he described an exciting experience and told how he felt about it. He decided to publish his poem as a poster.

Baseball

by Emanuel Campos

A batter hits the ball
And runs to first base.
The ball flies over the wall.
See the smile on his face.

Now it's time to publish your quatrain. Here are some ways you can share your poem with classmates, friends, and family members.

Make a Poster ▶

Design a poster around your poem. Draw colorful pictures, or cut out photos that go with your poem.

◀ Tape Your Poetry

As a class, produce an audiotape of your quatrains. Practice reading your poem out loud. Then read and record it. Add background music or sound effects.

What Type Are You? ▶

Some readers like fancy type. Others like old-fashioned type or simple type. Talk with your readers and find out what typefaces they like. Then print each one a special edition of your poem.

Writing a Comparison

How would you describe a dinosaur? Is it more like an elephant or a lizard? When you think about the similarities between two things, you are comparing them. A written **comparison**, like the one below, describes how two things are alike.

When Kenny Glazer visited a zoo, he realized that the lion cubs reminded him a lot of his cat, Cuddles. The more he thought about it, the more similarities he discovered. He wrote about the cats for school.

Meet the Writer

I like animals of all kinds. My kitten is named Cuddles. She's very much like the lion cub I saw at the zoo.

Kenny Glazer
Montana

Two Cats That Are Alike
by Kenny Glazer

Did you ever notice that kittens and lion cubs have a lot in common? I went to the zoo last Saturday. I looked into a cage and saw a lion cub. What a surprise! It looked a lot like my kitten, Cuddles. How are kittens and lion cubs alike?

Both Cuddles and the cub have nice soft fur and cute little tails. Both are very quiet when they move, although Cuddles seems to be quicker. Both Cuddles and the lion cub are very curious, too. They put their noses and paws into everything. That's not all they have in common. Both animals have claws and long whiskers. Both make a deep purring noise when they are happy.

You can see that kittens and lion cubs really are a lot alike, at least when they are young. The big difference is that when a lion grows up, I don't think it would be a very good pet for a nine-year-old boy.

Talk About the Model

★ How does the writer introduce the comparison?

★ How are lion cubs and kittens alike?

★ What words does the writer use to describe the two animals?

The first sentence introduces the two animals that are being compared.

The writer uses adjectives to compare the two animals.

Facts and supporting details tell how the two are alike.

The end sums up the information and gives the writer's opinion.

Hello!

From the ZOO

Make a Plan

Pick two things that you think are alike in some ways. They can be two people, animals, places, or objects. Then make a Venn diagram to explore the ways they are alike. In Kenny's diagram, the space where the circles overlap shows how cubs and kittens are alike.

Lion Cubs   My Kitten

claws
whiskers
curious
purrs
furry

Write It Down

- Begin with a topic sentence that names the two subjects you are comparing.
- Use details from the middle part of your Venn diagram. Show how the two subjects are similar.
- End by summing up your information.
- Give your comparison a title.

Conferencing

Share your writing with a partner or small group. Ask if the comparisons are clear. If your comparison didn't have a title, would readers still know what two things are being compared?

Look It Over

Reread your comparison aloud. Have you given enough facts and details? Did you use colorful adjectives and adverbs to make your comparison?

JUST THE FACTS

Writing to Inform

Writing an Informative Paragraph

Meet the Writer

My classmates and I got together to put on a play. It was such a big hit that a lot of the other kids wanted to know if they could put on a play, too.

Michael Reyes
Michigan

You know why plants grow. You know how to make pancakes. You even know how to program a VCR! You learned these things from writing that informs.

An **informative paragraph** gives readers facts and details about a topic. Michael's paragraph tells about putting on a play.

Our Class Play
by Michael Reyes

My class put on a play last week. We wrote it ourselves. It was about eating food that is good for us. We were going to put it on for the kindergarten class. First, we wrote the script. Then, we chose parts. We had to learn our parts by heart. We rehearsed for four days. The art teacher helped us with costumes. When we were ready, we put on the play for the kindergarten class. At the end, they all clapped. We had fun. I'd like to do it again!

Talk About the Model

★ What is the main idea of Michael's paragraph?

★ What details does he give to explain his main idea?

★ Do all the sentences tell about the main idea?

Make a Plan

Is there a topic you know a lot about? Could you tell about it in a paragraph? Here's your chance.

- First, brainstorm a list of topics.
- Share your list with your classmates. You may get an idea you hadn't thought of.
- Then, pick one topic. Make a cluster that shows what you could tell readers about your topic.

Write It Down

Once you have a topic and know what you want to say about it, you're ready to write.

- Begin your paragraph with a topic sentence. It should tell the main idea.
- Add facts and details in the next sentences.
- All the sentences should tell more about your main idea.

Conferencing

Read your paragraph to a partner. Ask if the main idea is clear. Do all the facts and details give information about the main topic? Is there anything else your partner would like to know?

Look It Over

Read your paragraph again. Is the main idea clear? Is your spelling and punctuation correct? Are the subject and verb in each sentence used correctly?

Writer's Tip
Write your topic sentence in a different color. That way, you will always know which sentence it is.

Portfolio
Put your paragraph in your portfolio. You might want to make it part of a longer piece of writing.

Writing an Interview

Are you curious about other people and what they know? If you are, you'll like writing an **interview.** In an interview you learn about a person or topic by asking questions.

In "Picturing the World," Allison Lassieur asked photographer Jodi Cobb questions about her life and work. Allison used Jodi's responses to write this magazine article.

Highlights for Children
Fun with a Purpose

The introduction identifies the person being interviewed.

Picturing the World
The Adventures of a Professional Photographer
by Allison Lassieur

Jodi Cobb is a photographer for *National Geographic* magazine. Since 1978 she has worked in more than twenty-five countries and taken thousands of pictures. She talked with *Highlights* about her experience.

What inspired you to become a photographer?

In my senior year of college I took a photography class. I discovered that photography is immediate—I could see the reaction when people looked at a photograph.

What do you do to prepare for an assignment?

I read as much as I can about a place and learn about local customs.

What strange foods have you eaten?

My most unusual meal was in a remote Chinese village where they brought me fried bumblebees.

Talk About the Model

As a Reader

★ Who is the subject of the interview? Why is Allison writing about her?

★ Which of Jodi's answers were the most interesting? Why?

As a Writer

★ How did the writer organize her information?

★ How do you think the writer decided what information to include?

What unusual kinds of transportation have you taken?

I've gone by camel in Jordan, by elephant in Thailand, and by icebreaker across the Baltic Sea.

Which did you like best?

Oh, I liked the camels. They make the most amazing noises when they walk.

How do you dress in different countries?

I try to dress as much like the people I'm photographing as possible.

How do you help people feel comfortable with you?

A smile and a respectful attitude go a long way. If you come in with genuine curiosity about their lives, people know it.

Questions and answers about the same subject are grouped together.

The person's words are quoted exactly.

The questions are in bold type.

Make a Plan

Choose Someone to Interview

First, think of a topic you would like to know more about. Then, ask yourself who you could talk to who knows about that topic. Maybe it's a relative, a friend, or someone in the community.

- Make a list of people you might interview.
- Choose someone who is interesting and knows a lot about your topic.

Tech Tip
Use **bold** type to set off your questions from the person's answers.

Make a List of Questions

- Write out your questions on paper. Leave space after each one to write answers.
- Begin questions with *how*, *what*, or *why*.

Conduct the Interview

- Bring your questions and a note pad or a tape recorder.
- Write down exactly what the person says.

Portfolio

Save your original interview notes in case you need to do additional revising.

Write It Down

- In the first paragraph, introduce the person you interviewed and identify the topic of your interview.
- Next, write your questions and answers.
- Use your notes to group questions and answers about the same topic together.

Conferencing

Share your interview with a partner. Ask if the information is clear. Is it in an order that makes sense?

Look It Over

Read your interview again. Did you identify your topic at the beginning?

Now You Know

How can you find out more about the things that interest you? Information can come from many sources, like friends, teachers, libraries, and the Internet. When you look up information and use it to write about a topic that interests you, you are writing a **research report.**

Meet the Writer

I saw a gray wolf named Coco at the zoo. I wanted to know more about wolves, so when we had to write a report, I chose gray wolves as my topic.

Jena Reider
Pennsylvania

A Research Report

★ Gives facts and details about a topic
★ Uses information from books, magazines, newspapers, and the Internet
★ Is based on notes that writers take in their own words
★ Has a beginning, middle, and end

Think It Through

Writing a research report may seem like a big job. When you break down the prewriting stage into small steps, it's much easier.

1. Brainstorm and select a topic.
2. Design a plan.
3. Look for information from different sources.
4. Organize your information.
5. Make an outline.

Brainstorm and Select a Topic

The first step is to find possible topics to write about. Jena knew she wanted to write about animals, but which ones? She looked through her journal and her social studies log for ideas. Then she made a chart to help her narrow her choices.

Jena had just been to the zoo, so she knew she could get information about the animals there. She decided to write about gray wolves.

animals

zoo animals

wild dogs

gray wolves

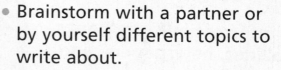

- Brainstorm with a partner or by yourself different topics to write about.
- A chart like Jena's can help you narrow your choice.
- Choose the topic you are most interested in learning about.

Design a Plan

First, Jena asked herself what she already knew about gray wolves. Then, she asked herself what questions she had about them. Jena put what she knew and what she wanted to know in a K-W-L chart. In the third column, she would write what she learned when she gathered information. Here is what her chart looked like.

WHAT I KNOW	WHAT I WANT TO KNOW	WHAT I LEARNED
The gray wolf is a wild dog. It is very fast.	How big is a gray wolf? How does it live? How does it hunt?	

Make a K-W-L chart like Jena's.

- In the first column, write what you already know about your topic.
- In the middle column, write some questions you want to answer when you go to the library.
- Write the answers to your questions in the third column.

Writer's Tip
Take your K-W-L chart to the library so that you can add to it as you learn more about your topic.

Portfolio

You will have many notes before you finish. Clip them together in your portfolio.

Look for Information

Your next step is to find information on your topic. Head for your school or public library first. If you need help finding information or using the computer, ask the librarian.

LIBRARIAN

PLACES TO GET INFORMATION
- books
- encyclopedias
- magazines
- CD-ROMs
- Internet

Use the Card or Computer Catalog

All the books in the library are listed in the **card catalog.** The cards are arranged in alphabetical order. There are usually three cards for every book.

Most libraries also have their card catalogs on a computer. Type in the title, author, or subject to find the book you want.

There are three cards for each book. They are organized by author, title, and subject.

WOLVES
j645   Anderson, Leigh
Ref   The Lives of Wolves. Illus. by J. Peters. Wildlife Press (c1999).

The Lives of Wolves
j645   Anderson, Leigh
Ref   The Lives of Wolves. Illus. by J. Peters. Wildlife Press (c1999).

j645   **Anderson, Leigh**
Ref   The Lives of Wolves. Illus. by J. Peters. Wildlife Press (c1999).
125 p. col. illus.
Information about the lives and habits of wolves, including the gray wolf. Discusses what they look like, where they live and what they eat. Glossary.
125 p. col. illus.

Each card shows the title, the author, illustrator, publisher, date, and number of pages.

A short description tells what the book is about.

Take Notes

The best way to remember the information you find is to take notes.

- Use one note card for each question from your K-W-L chart.

- At the top of the card, write where the information came from and the page number.

- Use your own words when you take notes.

If you find several facts in one place, you can write a short summary. For help in writing summaries, see pages 46–47.

Dogs, Dogs, Dogs, by C. Major, page 86
How big is a gray wolf?
The gray wolf is the largest wild dog.
It weighs more than 150 pounds.
It is more than 3 feet tall.

Tech Tip
The name of a Web site usually appears in a box at the top of your computer screen.

Begin your search for information in the library. In addition to books and magazines, don't forget CD-ROM encyclopedias and the Internet. Jena found some Web sites with photographs and information about gray wolves.

- Use the card or computer catalog to find books on your topic.

- Search on-line for more information.

- Use cards to take notes. Remember to include the name of your source and the page number.

Portfolio
Put a rubber band around your cards so that they don't get lost.

Organize Your Information

Jena found the answers to her questions in several books and on the Internet. She also found other information about gray wolves that she decided to include in her report.

To organize her information, she put all the cards with the same main idea into a pile. She ended up with three piles.

- What gray wolves look like
- How they live
- How they hunt

Sort your cards into piles, one for each main idea. If any of your piles have only one or two cards, you may want to go back to the library for more information.

Conferencing

Share your information with a partner. Ask if there is anything else about your topic you should include.

Make an Outline

Step 5

Jena used her note cards to create an outline for her report. An outline puts your ideas in order. Then, as you write, it helps you remember what you want to say. This is the outline that Jena made.

Roman numerals identify the main ideas. ••••▶

Capital letters identify each detail. •••••▶

Indent each capital letter and put a period after it. •••••▶

Information is written in phrases or single words ••••

The Gray Wolf

I. Introduction
II. What the gray wolf looks like
   A. Size
   B. Color
III. How the gray wolf lives
   A. Eats, sleeps, hunts in a pack
   B. Cubs
IV. Why it is a good hunter
   A. Runs fast
   B. Doesn't get tired
V. Conclusion
   A. Gray wolf is one kind of wild dog
   B. Other kinds

Your Turn

Use Jena's outline as a model to make your own.

- Include a title, an introduction, and a conclusion.
- Use Roman numerals for each main idea.
- Use capital letters for each detail under a main idea.

Conferencing

Share your outline with a partner. Ask if your main ideas are clear. Do you have enough details under each one? Have you left out any important information?

Tech Tip

Use a capital *I* and a capital *V* to make Roman numerals.

Portfolio

Put your outline on top when you put your notes and other materials away.

Drafting

Put It Into Words

Jena was excited about putting her ideas on paper. She had lots of interesting facts to tell. This is her first draft. What do you think of her topic?

Coco the Gray Wolf
by Jena Reider

The beginning introduces the topic.

Have you met Coco? She just arrived at the zoo. Coco is a gray wolf. Wolves are part of the wild dog family.

The middle gives facts and details.

It ways more than 150 pounds, and it is more than 3 foot tall. The gray wolf has gray-brown fur, pointed ears, and a bushy tail.

A pack is like a family. The wolves eat, sleep, and hunt together. Cubs stay with their parents until they can take care of themselves. Like other wild dogs, the gray wolf lives in a pack.

The gray wolf is a good hunter because the gray wolf can run very fast. It can go up to 40 miles an hour. It may keep running without getting tired.

The end sums up the information.

Wolves are only one kind of wild dog. Foxes coyotes jackals and dingoes are also in the wild dog family. If you want to learn more about wolves and other wild dogs, you can visit them all at the zoo.

Think Like a Writer

Here are some questions to think about as you write your first draft.

★ **Subject:** What do I want to know about my topic?

★ **Audience:** Who else will be interested in this information?

★ **Purpose:** What kind of information will my readers want to know?

★ **Form:** Have I followed all the steps in writing a research report?

Now you're all set to write. Use your note cards and outline to get your thoughts down on paper. This first draft does not have to be perfect. You'll have time later to make changes. Use the checklist to help you write your draft.

Drafting Checklist

- Follow your outline when you write, to keep your facts in order.
- The first paragraph identifies your topic.
- The middle part gives facts and details from books and other sources of information.
- The end sums up your main points.
- Give your report a title.

Conferencing

Talk about your draft with a partner. Ask if any part tells too much or too little about the topic. Is there any information that doesn't belong in your report?

Writer's Tip
Begin a new paragraph for each new main idea.

Tech Tip
Use the Return key to start a new paragraph. Use the Tab key to indent the first line.

Portfolio
Use a large envelope or paper clip to keep your outline, your note cards, and your first draft together.

Take Another Look

Jena liked her first draft. She thought it covered her main points. When she reread it, she decided to make some changes. How have her changes improved her research report?

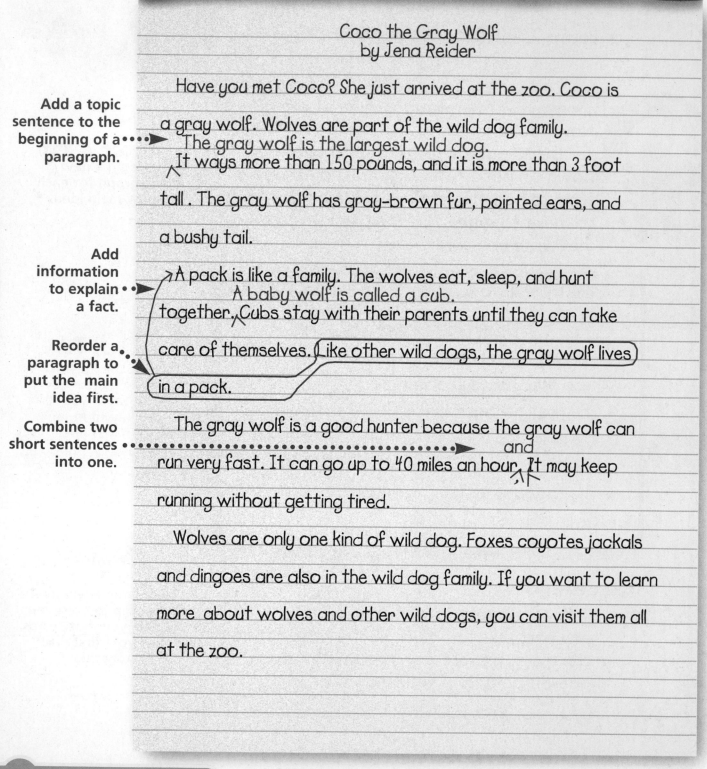

Coco the Gray Wolf
by Jena Reider

Have you met Coco? She just arrived at the zoo. Coco is a gray wolf. Wolves are part of the wild dog family. The gray wolf is the largest wild dog. It ways more than 150 pounds, and it is more than 3 foot tall. The gray wolf has gray-brown fur, pointed ears, and a bushy tail.

A pack is like a family. The wolves eat, sleep, and hunt together. A baby wolf is called a cub. Cubs stay with their parents until they can take care of themselves. Like other wild dogs, the gray wolf lives in a pack.

The gray wolf is a good hunter because the gray wolf can run very fast. It can go up to 40 miles an hour, and It may keep running without getting tired.

Wolves are only one kind of wild dog. Foxes coyotes jackals and dingoes are also in the wild dog family. If you want to learn more about wolves and other wild dogs, you can visit them all at the zoo.

Add a topic sentence to the beginning of a paragraph.

Add information to explain a fact.

Reorder a paragraph to put the main idea first.

Combine two short sentences into one.

It's your turn now to make the revisions you think are important. Read your first draft aloud. What do you like about it? What things need to be changed?

Make your changes right on your first draft. Use the Revising Checklist as your guide.

Revising Marks

≡ capitalize
∧ add
ℯ remove
⊙ add a period
/ make lowercase
◯ move
∼ transpose

Revising Checklist

- How does my report catch the reader's attention?
- Do I use facts and details to explain my main ideas?
- Is information on the same topic grouped together?
- Are my ideas presented in the best order?

Tech Tip

Remember to print out your file after you revise it.

Conferencing

Read your report to a partner. Tell why you made the changes you did. Are there any other changes you should make?

Portfolio

Keep all your drafts so that you can track your changes.

★ Become a Super Writer

Writers use catchy opening paragraphs to build readers' interest. For help, see page 219 in the *Writer's Handbook* section.

Polish Your Writing

When Jena edited and proofread her work, she found some mistakes. She was glad she caught them before she made her final copy. Did she miss any mistakes?

Coco the Gray Wolf
by Jena Reider

Have you met Coco? She just arrived at the zoo. Coco is a gray wolf. Wolves are part of the wild dog family.

Correct the spelling of a problem word. ⟶

The gray wolf is the largest wild dog. It ~~ways~~ *weighs* more than 150 pounds, and it is more than 3 ~~foot~~ *feet* tall. The gray wolf has gray-brown fur, pointed ears, and a bushy tail.

Use the correct plural form of a noun. ⟶

Like other wild dogs, the gray wolf lives in a pack. A pack is like a family. The wolves eat, sleep, and hunt together. A baby wolf is called a cub. Cubs stay with their parents until they can take care of themselves.

Change a noun to a pronoun. ⟶

The gray wolf is a good hunter because ~~the gray wolf~~ *it* can run very fast. It can go up to 40 miles an hour, and it ~~may~~ *can* keep running without getting tired.

Correct a problem word. ⟶

Wolves are only one kind of wild dog. Foxes, coyotes, jackals, and dingoes are also in the wild dog family. If you want to learn more about wolves and other wild dogs, you can visit them all at the zoo.

Add commas between words in a series. ⟶

Put on your editor's hat. It's time to make your final check before you publish your report. Use the Editing and Proofreading Checklist to help you. If you use a different-color pencil, your proofreading marks will stand out.

Proofreading Marks

Mark	Meaning
9	indent first line of paragraph
≡	capitalize
∧ or ∨	add
๑	remove
⊙	add a period
/	make lowercase
◯	spelling mistake
◡	move
∼	transpose

Editing and Proofreading Checklist

- Did I use commas correctly?

  See pages 256–258 in the *Writer's Handbook* section.

- Did I use nouns and pronouns correctly?

  See pages 244–246 in the *Writer's Handbook* section.

- Did I spell problem words correctly?

  See page 271 in the *Writer's Handbook* section.

Conferencing

Share your report with a partner. Ask if you spelled all the words correctly. Did you miss any mistakes?

Tech Tip

The Spelling tool cannot tell if you wrote *way* but meant *weigh*. Proofread your paper one last time.

Portfolio

Store your final copy inside your portfolio on top of your outline, note cards, and drafts.

Become a Super Writer

Watch out for word pairs like *way* and *weigh* that are easily confused. For help with problem words, see page 271 in the *Writer's Handbook* section.

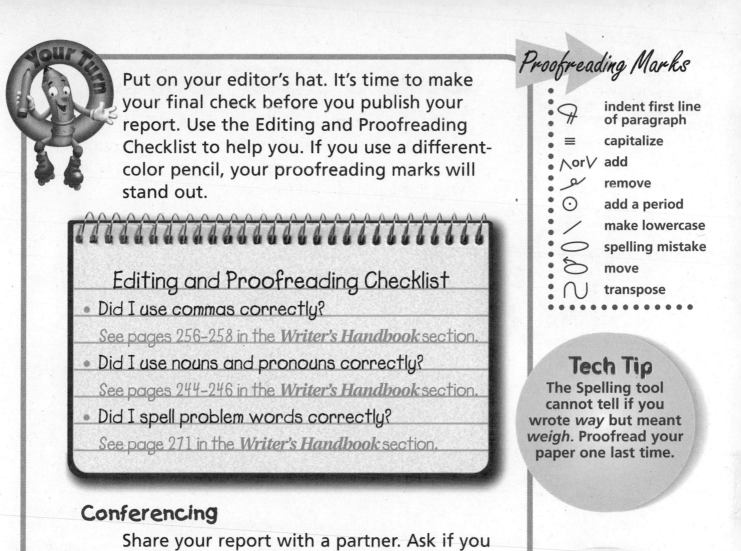

Share Your Work

After Jena made all her corrections, she printed out her report on the computer. She made a videotape of wolves at the zoo. She was looking forward to sharing what she learned with the class.

Coco the Gray Wolf
by Jena Reider

Have you met Coco? She just arrived at the zoo. Coco is a gray wolf. Wolves are part of the wild dog family.

The gray wolf is the largest wild dog. It weighs more than 150 pounds, and it is more than 3 feet tall. The gray wolf has gray-brown fur, pointed ears, and a bushy tail.

Like other wild dogs, the gray wolf lives in a pack. A pack is like a family. The wolves eat, sleep, and hunt together. A baby wolf is called a cub. Cubs stay with their parents until they can take care of themselves.

The gray wolf is a good hunter because it can run very fast. It can go up to 40 miles an hour, and it can keep running without getting tired.

Wolves are only one kind of wild dog. Foxes, coyotes, jackals, and dingoes are also in the wild dog family. If you want to learn more about wolves and other wild dogs, you can visit them all at the zoo.

Turn your classroom into an exciting "Class Information Center." Here are some suggestions on how to share your research reports.

Video Program ▶

Make a videotape about your topic. Jena went to the zoo to tape gray wolves. If you can't videotape your topic, have a friend make a video of you reading your report. You can even include pictures, photos, and charts.

◀ Reference Book

Publish your class's research reports as a reference book. Keep it in your classroom library. To prepare the book, have a committee make a table of contents and a "Meet the Author" section.

Meet the Author ▶

Organize a "Meet the Author" panel, starring the writers of the research reports. A moderator can ask writers to read their reports, talk about how they wrote them, and answer questions from the audience.

Writing a How-to Paragraph

Your little brother wants to know how to make a sandwich. Your best friend wants to know how to do a cartwheel. To answer them, you could write a **how-to paragraph**. A how-to paragraph gives directions for making or doing something.

In the article "Have a Balloon Blowout!" the writer gives clear, easy directions for playing games with balloons. Would you like to play?

Meet the Writer

Julie Vosburgh Agnone is a senior editor at *National Geographic World*, a kids' magazine published by the National Geographic Society.

To make sure the instructions were correct, I played the game. It made me feel like a kid again.

Talk About the Model

As a Reader

★ How is the paragraph organized?

★ Does the paragraph make you want to play Cling-ons? Why or why not?

As a Writer

★ How does the writer show the order of the steps?

★ Why is it helpful to have the materials listed in the beginning of the paragraph?

Have a Balloon Blowout!
by Julie Vosburgh Agnone

You'd be surprised at all the games you can play with balloons. One of my favorites is called Cling-ons. All you need are a group of kids, a lot of balloons, and a wall. First, blow up a pile of balloons and put them in the middle of a room. Next, divide kids into two teams, each assigned to work a different side of the room. At the word "go," players grab balloons from the pile and rub them on their hair to create static electricity. Then, each player tries to make the "electric" balloons stick to the wall. The team with the most balloons on the wall after three minutes wins.

The beginning introduces the topic and tells what you need to play.

Steps are given in order.

Directions are written in the present tense.

Make a Plan

Brainstorm a list of simple things you could tell someone how to do. Pick one that takes three or four steps to complete. You could write about how to wash the dog or fly a kite.

- Write your steps on index cards. Put each step on a separate card. If you have an idea for a picture, write it on the card for the step it goes with.

- Decide on the best order for your steps. Then number the cards in the correct order.

Write It Down

- Identify your topic in the opening sentence. Make readers interested in what they will do.

- Include a list of materials or ingredients that will be needed.

- Picture each step in your mind. Explain each one in order.

- Follow the steps on your index cards. Write short, simple sentences. Words like *first*, *next,* and *last* will help tell the order.

Tech Tip

The Cut and Paste tools make it easy to change the order of your steps.

Conferencing

Ask a partner to actually do each step or to pantomime doing the steps exactly as you wrote them. Are the steps clear?

Portfolio

Save your how-to paragraph in case you want to use your instructions at another time.

Look It Over

Double-check to see if your steps are in the right order. Did you use the correct verb tense throughout your article?

Is There a Letter for Me?

If you send mail, you'll get mail. A letter written to a friend or relative is called a **friendly letter.** It is a very personal way to share news and feelings. Invitations and thank-you notes are also friendly letters.

A Friendly Letter

★ Tells what's happening in the writer's life

★ Begins with a **heading** that gives the writer's address and the date

★ Has a **greeting** that usually begins with *Dear* and the person's name

★ Includes a **body,** or main part, that tells the writer's activities and ideas

★ Ends with a **closing,** such as *Your friend,* and the writer's **signature,** or name

Meet the Writer

I sent this letter to my friend Justin. I can't wait to hear what he says about our trip. He likes snakes and bugs as much as I do.

Chace Michaylira
Florida

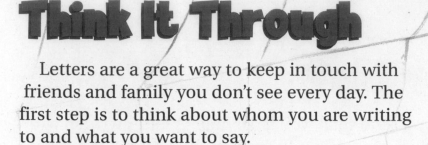

Think It Through

Letters are a great way to keep in touch with friends and family you don't see every day. The first step is to think about whom you are writing to and what you want to say.

Brainstorming

Chace often writes to his best friend, Justin, who moved away last year. Chace had a lot to tell Justin. He made a list of things he had done recently.

CHACE'S LIST

WHAT I DID

1. played baseball
2. saw a school play
3. went to the park
4. tried out for soccer team

WHAT HAPPENED

1. caught a fly ball
2. my brother forgot his lines
3. saw a snake swallow a toad
4. made the Blue Team

First, decide whom you are writing to. Maybe you have a friend who lives in another state or a relative you don't see very often. Then, make a list like Chace's to help you decide what to write about.

Select a Topic

Chace decided to write about the trip to the park and the soccer team. He knew Justin would be interested in both of them.

- Circle the topics you want to write about.
- Keep your reader's interests in mind. Circle the topics your reader would want to hear about.
- Are there any topics with two circles around them? They're the best ones!

Design a Plan

Once Chace knew what he wanted to tell Justin, he made a chart of topics and details so that he wouldn't forget anything when he started writing.

TOPIC	DETAILS
Trip to Erna Nixon Park	1. saw butterflies and animal tracks
	2. watched snake swallow toad
	3. stepped in poison ivy
Summer visit	1. hope you can come again this summer
	2. found a silk spider
Soccer	1. playing on the Blue Team
	2. scored two goals

Your Turn

Make your own chart to help organize your ideas. Use Chace's as a model.

In the left column, write the topic. In the right column, list the details you want to include.

Conferencing

Show your chart to a partner. Are the main points clear? Should you add or take out any details?

Portfolio

Save your list and chart and use them when you write your first draft.

Put It Into Words

Chace kept his list and chart nearby as he began to write. Following the form of a friendly letter, he wrote his address and the date first. Do you remember what this is called?

The heading includes the writer's address and date.

> 26 Palm Rd
> melbourne, FL 32935
> April 22, 1999

The greeting opens the letter.

dear Justin,

The body is the main part of the letter. It includes the main ideas and details.

Last week, all of the third grade went on a field trip to Erna Nixon Park. At first, all we saw were some butterflies and some animal tracks. We saw a snake on a rock. The snake swallowed a whole toad! I was trying to get closer so I could see. I steped in poison ivy.

I hope you can come visit next summer. We can hunt for insects and reptiles again. Last summer we saw a silk spider spinning its web. That was the coolest spider.

Are you playing soccer this year? I'm on the Blue Team.

The closing ends the letter with a friendly goodbye.

I scored two goals in our first game.

Your friend

The signature is the writer's name.

Chace

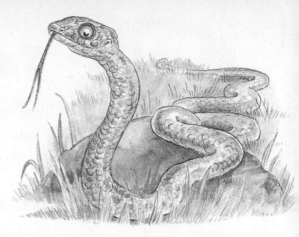

Think Like a Writer

As you write your first draft, think about

★ **Subject:** What events or news am I writing about?

★ **Audience:** Who will be interested in reading this?

★ **Purpose:** What information can I give that will get the reader to write back?

★ **Form:** What are the parts of a friendly letter?

Your Turn

Once your thoughts are in order, write your draft. Remember, corrections will come later. Look at the Drafting Checklist before and after you write.

Drafting Checklist

- The letter has information about what's happening in your life.
- The letter holds the reader's interest by asking questions.
- The body of the letter has a paragraph for each topic, which includes details and facts.
- The letter follows the correct format: heading, greeting, body, closing, and signature.
- The language is friendly and fun, since it's a letter to a friend or relative.

Conferencing

Ask a partner to look over your first draft. Have you included all the parts of a friendly letter? Take notes as you listen.

Take Another Look

Chace read over his first draft. He decided to make some changes that would make his writing clearer and more interesting. What do you think of his changes?

26 Palm Rd
melbourne, FL 32935
April 22, 1999

dear Justin,

Add a detail about the park. ●●●●● ►   Last week, all of the third grade went on a field trip to
It's a huge park with a lake and woods around it.
Erna Nixon Park. At first, all we saw were some butterflies

Add a word to make the order of events clearer. ●●●●●●●●●●● ►   ∧   Then,
and some animal tracks. We saw a snake on a rock. The
∧

snake swallowed a whole toad! I was trying to get closer

Combine two short sentences into one. ●●●●●●●●●● ►   and
so I could see, I steped in poison ivy.
∧

Change a sentence into a question to vary the kind of sentences. ●●●●●●●●●●●●●●●●●● ►   I hope you can come visit next summer. We can hunt for
Do you remember when
insects and reptiles again. Last summer we saw a silk spider
?   ∧

spinning its web, That was the coolest spider.
∧

Are you playing soccer this year? I'm on the Blue Team.

Change the beginning of a sentence to avoid repetition. ●●● ►   I scored two goals in our first game.
∧

Your friend

Chace

Read your letter over and think about the person who will be receiving it. Will everything be clear? Does anything need to be changed? Refer to the Revising Checklist for other ideas about what to change.

Revising Marks

≡	capitalize
∧	add
℘	remove
⊙	add a period
/	make lowercase
⊘	move
∾	transpose

Revising Checklist

- Are there enough details to make this letter interesting?
- Is the order of events clear?
- Are different kinds of sentences used?
- Do the sentences begin in different ways?
- Are the sentences different lengths?
- Does the letter follow the correct format?

Conferencing

Get together with a partner. Go over the questions on the Revising Checklist. What kinds of revisions should you make?

Tech Tip
Use the Cut and Paste tools to move words and sentences.

Portfolio

Keep magazine articles, drawings, or anything else your friend might be interested in to include with future letters.

Become a Super Writer

To make your writing more interesting, use different kinds and lengths of sentences. Also, begin sentences in different ways. For help, see page 221 in the *Writer's Handbook* section.

POISON IVY

Polish Your Writing

Chace put a lot of effort into writing this friendly letter. He gave it a final proofreading before he was ready to mail it.

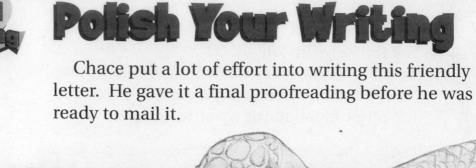

Add a period at the end of an abbreviation. ·····▶

Capitalize the name of a city. ·····▶

26 Palm Rd.

melbourne, FL 32935
April 22, 1999

Capitalize the greeting of a letter. ····▶

dear Justin,

    Last week, all of the third grade went on a field trip to

Erna Nixon Park. It's a huge park with a lake and woods

around it. At first, all we saw were some butterflies and

some animal tracks. Then, we saw a snake on a rock.

The snake swallowed a whole toad! I was trying to get

stepped

Correct a spelling mistake. ·····▶

closer so I could see, and I (steped) in poison ivy.

    I hope you can come visit next summer. We can hunt for

Add an exclamation point at the end of a sentence. ·····▶

insects and reptiles again. Do you remember when we saw a

silk spider spinning its web? That was the coolest spider!

    Are you playing soccer this year? I'm on the Blue Team. In

our first game, I scored two goals.

Put a comma after the closing of a letter. ·····▶

Your friend,

Chace

Are you ready to put the final touches on your letter? Carefully edit and proofread it. Use the Editing and Proofreading Checklist to help you.

Proofreading Marks

¶	indent first line of paragraph
≡	capitalize
∧ or ∨	add
✄	remove
⊙	add a period
/	make lowercase
○	spelling mistake
⟋	move
∼	transpose

Editing and Proofreading Checklist

- Did I indent each paragraph?
  See page 253 in the *Writer's Handbook* section.
- Did I capitalize proper nouns in the heading of my letter?
  See pages 248–250 in the *Writer's Handbook* section.
- Did I capitalize the first word in the greeting and closing?
  See page 251 in the *Writer's Handbook* section.
- Did I put a comma after the greeting and the closing?
  See page 257 in the *Writer's Handbook* section.
- Did I spell all the words correctly?
  See pages 262–271 in the *Writer's Handbook* section.

Conferencing

Share your letter with a partner. Ask your partner to check for spelling mistakes. Did you remember to capitalize proper nouns?

Tech Tip
Remember to use the Shift key to capitalize a letter.

Portfolio
Store your notes, revisions, and final draft until you are ready to mail your letter.

Become a Super Writer

There are a lot of words that should be capitalized in the heading, greeting, and closing of a letter. Did you get them all? For help, see the *Writer's Handbook* section, page 251.

Share Your Work

Chace made his final corrections. Before he printed out his final copy, he added a border and some clip art of a soccer player to his letter. How do you think Justin will like Chace's letter?

26 Palm Rd.
Melbourne, FL 32935
April 22, 1999

Dear Justin,
    Last week, all of the third grade went on a field trip to Erna Nixon Park. It's a huge park with a lake and woods around it. At first, all we saw were some butterflies and some animal tracks. Then, we saw a snake on a rock. The snake swallowed a whole toad! I was trying to get closer so I could see, and I stepped in poison ivy.
    I hope you can come visit next summer. We can hunt for insects and reptiles again. Do you remember when we saw a silk spider spinning its web? That was the coolest spider!
    Are you playing soccer this year? I'm on the Blue Team. In our first game, I scored two goals.

Your friend,
Chace

Chace Michaylira
26 Palm Rd.
Melbourne, FL 32935

Justin Lucas
2234 Alta Vista Dr.
Newport Beach, CA 92660

Mail Your Letter ▶

Now it's time to address your envelope. Use Chace's envelope as a model for your own.

- Put your name and address in the upper left-hand corner of the envelope.
- Put the name and address of the person receiving the letter in the middle of the envelope.
- Put a stamp in the upper right-hand corner.

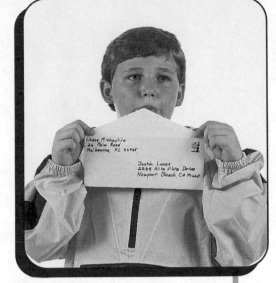

◀ E-mail

Are you in a hurry? Send your letter electronically, or by E-mail. Both you and the person you're writing to must have a computer, access to the Internet, and an E-mail address. The best thing about E-mail is that it's delivered as soon as you send it.

Video Mail ▶

If you have a video camera, have a friend videotape you while you read your letter. Mail the tape in a sturdy envelope. Be sure to include enough postage.

Writing a Book Report

Meet the Writer

I've read ten books by this author. The great thing about books in a series is that when you finish one, there's always another one to read.

Melanie James
Ohio

How do you decide which book to read? Do you read the words written about the book on the cover? Do you talk with friends and family members?

One of the best ways to a find a good book is to read a **book report.** A book report is a summary that tells about the characters, setting, and plot of a story. Most writers tell about books they really like and think other people would like, too.

A Book Report on The Mystery of the Hot Air Balloon
by Melanie James

The Mystery of the Hot Air Balloon by Gertrude Chandler Warner is one of the Boxcar Children Mysteries. Benny, Violet, Jessie, and Henry Alden are orphans. They live with their grandfather. Like other books in this series, the children solve mysteries.

In this story, the Aldens meet a man and a woman who fly hot-air balloons. They want to put on a hot-air balloon show in a small town called Lloyds Landing. Suddenly, things start to go wrong. Someone in town doesn't want the show to be there and tries to ruin it.

I can't tell you what happens. You'll have to read the book to find out how the mystery is solved. This is the best of all the Boxcar Children books I've read so far.

Talk About the Model

★ Do you think the writer did a good job of summarizing the book? Why or why not?

★ How does the writer feel about the book?

★ Does the writer make you want to read the book? Explain your answer.

The title, author, and type of book are identified in the beginning.

The characters and setting are introduced.

The main events are briefly described.

The ending of the book is not given away.

The writer's opinion encourages others to read the book.

Make a Plan

Choose a Book to Write About

You've just read a great book. In fact, you hope there are some others by the same author. Now you want to share your excitement with your friends by writing a book report.

- Think about your audience. Who will your readers be?
- Remember that the purpose of a book report is to summarize information about the characters, setting, and story and to give your opinion of the book.

Organize Your Information

To organize her thoughts, Melanie made an outline of important points to cover in her book report. Use Melanie's outline as a model to make your own outline.

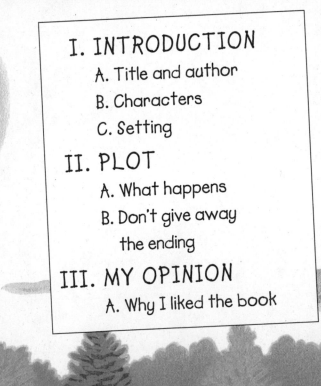

I. INTRODUCTION
    A. Title and author
    B. Characters
    C. Setting

II. PLOT
    A. What happens
    B. Don't give away
       the ending

III. MY OPINION
    A. Why I liked the book

Write It Down

Before you begin to write, think about your audience and purpose for writing. Follow your outline as you write. Don't forget to include details that will keep your readers interested.

Facts First

- Tell the title and author of the book in the first sentence. Underline the title.
- Briefly describe the characters and the setting.

Don't Give Away the Ending

- Tell the main events of the story in the order that they happened.
- Don't tell how the story ends.

What Do You Think?

- Tell why you liked the book.
- Encourage your audience to read the book.

Conferencing

Read your book report to a small group of classmates. What do they think? Take notes on any suggestions they make. Think about how to use their suggestions to make your report better.

Tech Tip

On a computer, you can use italics for the title of a book instead of underlining it.

Portfolio

Set up a special book report section in your portfolio so that you can exchange book reports with your classmates.

Look It Over

Imagine that the author of the book will see your report. Would the author like your report? Does the language of your report match your purpose and audience? Did you underline the title of the book and capitalize the first letter of each important word?

Share Your Work

Book reports are made to be shared with friends and classmates. Here are some different ways to publish them.

Author Day

Have you and your classmates written about books by the same author? Have an Author Day! Gather some information about the author and present it along with your book reports. Display all your reports together, with a photo or drawing of the author.

Book Jackets

Make book jackets for the books you reviewed. Illustrate the front cover and put your review on the back.

IN MY OPINION

Writing to Persuade

Writing a Persuasive Paragraph

Meet the Writer

I think everybody should join the Brownie Club. We have fun and we help the school. I like it so much I wrote this paragraph to convince other kids to join.

Cheryl Martin
Missouri

Is there something you really enjoy doing? How would you convince a friend to join you? A **persuasive paragraph** tells how the writer feels about something and gives reasons why. The point is to get the reader to agree with the writer. In "Brownies for Sale," Cheryl describes an activity that is lots of fun and also helps her school. She wants everybody to join the Brownie Club.

Brownies for Sale

by Cheryl Martin

I think everyone should join the Brownie Club. It's fun to bake brownies. It's even more fun to sell them! Ms. Reynolds helps us on Wednesdays after school. I like learning how to bake. I've met a lot of new friends. We sell our brownies at lunch on Thursdays. The money we raise pays for our class trips. The best part is afterward, when we get to eat the leftovers. Where else can you have fun and help your school, too?

Talk About the Model

- Where does the writer tell what the paragraph is about?

- What reasons does the writer give to join the Brownie Club?

Make a Plan

Now it's your turn to write. Start by making a list of things you like to do or feel strongly about.

- Think about things at home, in school, and in your community.

- Choose the one you care about the most.

- Make a list of reasons why you feel the way you do.

Tech Tip

Choose a larger type size than usual if you want to display your paragraph.

Write It Down

- In your first sentence, identify your topic and tell how you feel about it.

- Give two or three reasons why you feel that way.

- Use personal pronouns such as *I* and *me* to tell how you feel about your topic.

Portfolio

Keep your notes and paragraph in your portfolio. You may want to make them into a poster someday.

Conferencing

Read your paragraph to a partner. Ask if your reasons are convincing. Take notes if your partner makes suggestions.

Look It Over

Read your paragraph again. Do you need to add any information to make your opinion clear? Did you use the personal pronouns *I* and *me* correctly?

Writing a Brochure

Visiting a new place is great fun, even if it's only for a day. But how do you decide where to go and what to see? A **brochure** might help you. A brochure uses words and pictures to tell the reader about an interesting place to visit.

This is a brochure about the National Aquarium in Baltimore, Maryland. It was written to let people know about all the exciting fish they can see there and to encourage people to visit.

Meet the Writers

Not everything is written by just one writer. This brochure is the work of a team of writers, photographers, artists, and designers. It took all of their ideas and work to produce this brochure.

The topic is identified at the beginning.

Interesting titles catch the reader's attention.

Experience the Magic of the National Aquarium

Colorful reef fish, sleek sharks, and electric eels are just a few of the amazing fish you can see at the aquarium.

Sea It All

Explore the four corners of the globe in one place. See clownfish in a coral reef and piranhas in the rivers of the rain forest.

Magnificent Mammals of the Sea

Fish aren't the only animals that live in the sea. Visit the Marine Mammal Pavilion and watch graceful dolphins leap and play. Learn about other marine mammals at the Exploration Station, a special hands-on exhibit.

NATIONAL AQUARIUM IN BALTIMORE

Talk About the Model

As a Reader

★ What catches your attention first when you look at the brochure?

★ What do the pictures tell you about the aquarium?

As a Writer

★ What are some of the reasons the writer gives for visiting the aquarium?

★ How does the writer use words to make the aquarium sound like a place you would want to visit?

Jungle of Life

Follow a winding path through a tropical rain forest. Look carefully. Hiding in the trees are golden tamarinds, emerald-green iguanas, and ever-so-slow sloths.

Vivid, descriptive words create a picture for the reader.

What's New

Coming soon to the aquarium:

• a colorful display of exotic poisonous animals
• an exciting new dolphin program

The photographs make it look fun and exciting.

Make a Plan

The first step is to choose a place to write about. Think about different places you've been to on vacation or for the day. What interesting places are right in your own town?

Where Would You Like to Visit?

Make a chart and list as many places as you can think of. Your journal or the social studies section of your Learning Log may give you some ideas. Use the chart below as a model.

Places I've Been	Places I'd Like to Go	Places Nearby
1.	1.	1.
2.	2.	2.
3.	3.	3.

When you finish your chart, choose one place you would like to write about.

Why Do You Want to Go There?

The next step is to list the reasons you think people should visit the place you've chosen.

- Make a list of your reasons.
- Choose the three or four best ones.
- Circle the most important reason.

Design Your Brochure

Now it's time to think about how your brochure will look. A four-page brochure is a good length.

- Make a sketch of where you want the title, text, and pictures to go on each page.
- Do you have enough information? If not, use the library or the Internet.
- Take photographs, draw pictures, or cut pictures from a magazine.

Tech Tip
Use clip art, a fancy typeface, and page borders to dress up your brochure.

Write It Down

Now you're ready to put words and pictures together.

Catch Your Readers' Attention

- Give your brochure an interesting title.
- Include the name and location of the place.

Keep Them Interested

- On the inside pages, give reasons why people should visit. Make your location sound exciting.
- Include a photo or picture with each reason. Write captions.
- Use headings and titles to grab the readers' attention.
- Use colorful descriptive words.

Writer's Tip
Make sure your lettering is large and clear enough to be read easily.

Give Enough Information

- Tell your readers what they can see and do when they visit. Let them know about new exhibits and special events.
- Include the address and phone number so they can get more information.

Conferencing

Ask a partner if the words and pictures in your brochure work well together. Have you given readers good reasons to visit? Have you included enough information?

Look It Over

Read your brochure. Have you used enough descriptive words? Did you use suffixes correctly?

Portfolio

Keep your notes and sketches in your portfolio. Compare them with your finished brochure.

Share Your Work

Turn your classroom into a travel agency. Here are some ideas.

Travel Agents

Become a travel agent. Encourage classmates to visit the place you wrote about. Describe the place and answer questions about it. You may even want to make copies of your brochure to hand out.

Air Time

Videotape a short TV commercial for the place you wrote about. Use your brochure as a starting point and show it while you talk.

Class Travel Guide

Divide the class's brochures into "In Town," "Day Trip," and "Far Away." Then display them or mount them in a binder. The binder can be kept in your class library as a travel guide.

Read Any Good Books?

There are so many books to choose from. How do you know what to read next? A **book review** might help. A book review tells about the characters, setting, and main events of a story. It also tells what the writer thought of the book and gives reasons why.

A Book Review

★ Includes the title and name of the author

★ Describes the setting and the main characters

★ Briefly retells the story's main events

★ Gives the writer's opinion of the book

★ Gives reasons and examples to support the writer's opinion

Meet the Writer

Chris Van Allsburg is one of my favorite authors. I liked *The Sweetest Fig* because it is both real and make-believe. I'd like to be able to write like that.

Logan Takahashi
New Jersey

Think It Through

Have you read any good books lately? Is there one you think your classmates would enjoy? The first step in writing a book review is to choose a book.

Brainstorming

Think about books you've read recently. Check your Literature Log or your journal for ideas. Logan made a list of all the books he had read since school started.

Books I've Read

The Mystery of the Hot Air Balloon
The Not-So-Jolly Roger
The Sweetest Fig

> **Your Turn**
>
> Make a list of the books you've read. If you have trouble remembering them all, talk to your classmates. Chances are, you've read many of the same books.

Select a Topic

Now you need to choose a book to write about. As you look at your list, ask yourself

- why did I like this book?
- would I read it again?
- how can I convince my friends to read this book?

Design a Plan

There were a lot of things Logan liked about *The Sweetest Fig.* He knew if he could convince the other kids, they would like the book as much as he did. To organize his thoughts, Logan made a chart of the information he wanted to include in his review.

Book:	<u>The Sweetest Fig</u>
Author:	Chris Van Allsburg
Characters:	Bibot, Marcel, the old lady
Setting:	Paris, France
What happens:	An old lady gives Bibot, the dentist, two magic figs. When he eats them, his dreams will come true. He eats the first one, and his dream does come true. When he goes to eat the second one, something surprising happens.
What I think about the book: Why?	It's one of my favorites. 1. The story is both real and make-believe. 2. The ending is a surprise.

Your Turn

Make a chart like Logan's to plan your book review.
- Tell what you thought of the book.
- Give two reasons why you feel the way you do.
- Include examples from the story.

Conferencing

Discuss your plan with a partner. Review the characteristics of a book review on page 179. Have you included the reasons why you liked the book?

Portfolio

If possible, keep a copy of the book in your classroom near your portfolio.

Put It Into Words

Logan knew what he wanted to say about the story, and he had good reasons why he'd recommend this book to his friends. Now, he was ready to write.

The title and author are identified.

The writer gives his opinion of the book.

The characters and setting are described.

The main events are described in the order that they happened.

He also gives reasons for his opinion.

A Book Review of
The Sweetest Fig
by Logan Takahashi

The Sweetest Fig by Chris Van Allsburg is one of my

favorite books. The story is about Bibot, a dentist, and his

dog, Marcel. They live in Paris France. One day an old lady

comes to Bibot to have her tooth pulled. When he finishes,

she gives him two magic figs that will make his dreams come

true. Bibot eats one of the figs. You won't believe

what happens. It was just like in his dream.

If you like stories that are real and make-believe, you

should read The Sweetest Fig. Bibot and Marcel could be

reel. The magic figs and what happens to Bibot are

make-believe — and very funny.

The best part of the book is the ending.

The end is a surprise.

Think Like a Writer As you write your first draft, keep these points in mind.

★ **Subject:** What book am I writing about?

★ **Audience:** Who will read my book review?

★ **Purpose:** How can I tell readers what a great book this is?

★ **Form:** What information do I need to include?

You're ready to write your book review. Follow your outline and write your first draft. There will be time to make changes later. These guidelines will help you.

Drafting Checklist

- Include the name of the book and the author.
- Briefly tell about the book's main characters, setting, and story.
- Tell the events in the order that they happened. Don't give away the ending.
- Tell what you thought of the book.
- Give reasons for your opinion.

Conferencing

Share your review with a partner. Would he or she read the book based on your review. Why or why not?

Writer's Tip
Before you start to write, skim through the book quickly. It will help refresh your memory.

Tech Tip
Use italics for the title of the book instead of underlining it.

Portfolio
Clip together your draft, outline, and conferencing notes.

Take Another Look

When Logan reread his draft, he remembered some details he wanted to add. He also added a sentence to show how much he liked the book. How do these changes improve his book review?

Add a sentence explaining the writer's opinion of the book.

Add words to make order of events clearer.

Add a detail about the story.

Add a descriptive word.

Add a sentence to persuade the reader.

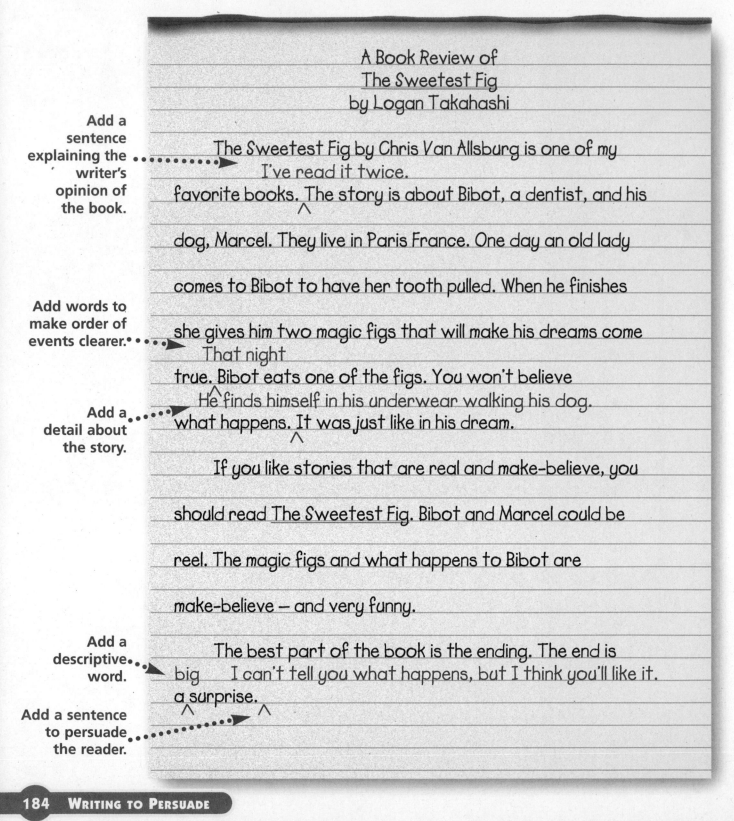

A Book Review of
The Sweetest Fig
by Logan Takahashi

The Sweetest Fig by Chris Van Allsburg is one of my
I've read it twice.
favorite books. The story is about Bibot, a dentist, and his
∧

dog, Marcel. They live in Paris France. One day an old lady

comes to Bibot to have her tooth pulled. When he finishes

she gives him two magic figs that will make his dreams come
That night
true. Bibot eats one of the figs. You won't believe
∧
He finds himself in his underwear walking his dog.
what happens. It was just like in his dream.
∧

If you like stories that are real and make-believe, you

should read The Sweetest Fig. Bibot and Marcel could be

reel. The magic figs and what happens to Bibot are

make-believe — and very funny.

The best part of the book is the ending. The end is
big   I can't tell you what happens, but I think you'll like it.
a surprise.
∧   ∧

Read your book review to yourself. Did you follow your plan? Use the Revising Checklist to help you decide if you need to make any changes.

Revising Marks

≡   capitalize

∧   add

⌿   remove

⊙   add a period

/   make lowercase

◠   move

∼   transpose

Revising Checklist

- Are there enough details about the characters, the setting, and the story to interest my readers?
- Is the order of events clear?
- Is my opinion of the book clearly stated?
- Do I give enough reasons for my opinion?

Tech Tip
Keep copies of all your drafts on your hard drive. Label them by number and date.

Conferencing

Read your revised draft to your partner. Ask if the main events are described clearly. Is there anything else you should add?

Portfolio
Store your revised work in your portfolio for the final stages of editing and proofreading.

Become a Super Writer

Details bring your writing alive and help create a picture for the reader. For help, see the *Writer's Handbook* section, page 210.

Logan read his revised draft carefully. He saw that there were some small corrections he still needed to make. Did he miss any mistakes?

A Book Review of
The Sweetest Fig
by Logan Takahashi

Underline the title of a book. ······► The Sweetest Fig by Chris Van Allsburg is one of my

favorite books. I've read it twice. The story is about

Add a comma between a city and country. ·············► Bibot, a dentist, and his dog, Marcel. They live in Paris France.
                                                                                                          ʌ,

One day an old lady comes to Bibot to have her tooth pulled.

Add a comma after introductory words. ·········► When he finishes she gives him two magic figs that will make
                                                                     ʌ,

his dreams come true. That night Bibot eats one of the

                                                                                    !
figs. You won't believe what happens,⸮He finds himself in his
                                                                             ʌ

Correct the punctuation at the end of a sentence. ········► underwear walking his dog. It was just like in his dream.

If you like stories that are real and make-believe, you

Correct a spelling mistake. ···► real
should read The Sweetest Fig. Bibot and Marcel could be
(reel) The magic figs and what happens to Bibot are

make-believe — and very funny.

The best part of the book is the ending. The end is a big

surprise. I can't tell you what happens, but I think you'll like it.

Now it's time for you to be your own editor and proofreader! Read your book review carefully. Use the Proofreading Marks and the checklist to help you.

Proofreading Marks

⌐	indent first line of paragraph
≡	capitalize
∧ or ∨	add
℘	remove
⊙	add a period
/	make lowercase
◌	spelling mistake
◌	move
∾	transpose

Editing and Proofreading Checklist

- Did I use commas correctly?

  See pages 256–258 in the *Writer's Handbook* section.

- Did I underline or italicize the title of my book?

  See page 259 in the *Writer's Handbook* section.

- Did I spell the words correctly?

  See pages 262–271 in the *Writer's Handbook* section.

Conferencing

Share your book review with a partner. Does your review convince your partner to read the book?

Tech Tip

Make a cover for your book review. Use a special typeface for the title.

Portfolio

Store your final draft in your folder until publication time.

Become a Super Writer

Commas can help make your writing clearer. For help, see the *Writer's Handbook* section, pages 256–258.

My Book Review
by L. Takahashi

A+

Share Your Work

Logan printed out a final copy of his book review. Then he drew the cover of the book on posterboard so he could share it with other classes. Does his review make you want to read *The Sweetest Fig*?

A Book Review of
The Sweetest Fig
by Logan Takahashi

The Sweetest Fig by Chris Van Allsburg is one of my favorite books. I've read it twice. The story is about Bibot, a dentist, and his dog, Marcel. They live in Paris, France. One day an old lady comes to Bibot to have her tooth pulled. When he finishes, she gives him two magic figs that will make his dreams come true. That night Bibot eats one of the figs. You won't believe what happens! He finds himself in his underwear walking his dog. It was just like in his dream.

If you like stories that are real and make-believe, you should read *The Sweetest Fig*. Bibot and Marcel could be real. The magic figs and what happens to Bibot are make-believe — and very funny.

The best part of the book is the ending. The end is a big surprise. I can't tell you what happens, but I think you'll like it.

Here are some suggestions for publishing your book review.

Books on Parade ▶

On a large sheet of posterboard, make a cover for the book you reviewed. Draw or paint an illustration and write the title of the book and the author in large letters. Have everyone carry their book covers and go in a parade to other classes.

◀ Book Talk

Star in your own radio show. Choose someone to be the interviewer and to ask you questions about the book you reviewed. You can tell about the book and give your opinion of it. Tape-record the interview.

Books Alive ▶

Act out a scene from your book. Gather a group of classmates who have also read the book and give each one a part. Read from the book or write your own script and put on a skit for the class.

Writing an Advertisement

Imagine that you invented a great new product. How would you get people to buy it? The best way would be to write an **advertisement**, or ad. An advertisement uses pictures and words to encourage people to do something or buy something.

Someone in an ad agency came up with the idea of putting "milk mustaches" on athletes, actors, and celebrities to sell more milk.

Ads like this one for milk are created by a group of people in an advertising agency. Creating a great ad takes the talents of copywriters, artists, photographers, and designers all working together.

My daughter has my eyes. And my smile. Well...almost. She also shares my love of milk. On ice, of course. Which could come in handy, considering the calcium helps give us something every skater needs. Strong ankles.

MILK
Where's *your* mustache?

Talk About the Model

As a Reader

★ What first grabs your attention in these ads? Why?

★ Is the written information interesting? Why or why not?

As a Writer

★ What reasons do the ads give for drinking milk?

★ Why do you think the writers use famous people in the pictures?

Have you seen me sweat? I must lose 10 pounds a game. And from what I hear, it's not just about losing water. It's about nutrients. That's why I drink milk, 2%. It's got nine essential nutrients my body needs, like calcium and potassium. I thought about telling my boys in Chicago, but it's about time they lost something.

MILK
Where's your mustache?

A photograph with an unusual feature catches the reader's attention.

Reasons are given to persuade the reader.

A question at the end catches the reader's attention.

Make a Plan

Think about something you want to advertise. It can be a car wash or another event. It can be a service you offer, such as walking dogs for people. It can even be a new product you dreamed up.

- Make a list of reasons why someone would need this product or service.

- Next, make a list of adjectives you could use to describe your product or service.

- Think about how you could illustrate your ad.

Writer's Tip
Good ads say a lot in a few words. Make every word count.

Write It Down

- Catch the reader's attention. Be sure people know what the product or service is.

- In the body of the ad, give two or three reasons why people would want this product.

- Use colorful, vivid adjectives. Keep your sentences short and to the point.

- Add an eye-catching illustration.

Tech Tip
Try mixing different sizes and styles of type for title and text.

Conferencing

Share your ad with a partner. Ask if the subject is clear. Are your reasons convincing? Did the ad catch your partner's attention?

Look It Over

Review your purpose, audience, and form. Do they work together? Are proper names and titles capitalized?

Portfolio
Keep your final copy. You may want to display it or use it as a model for another ad.

Dear Mr. Kerman...

Have you ever bought something only to find that it was broken or didn't work? When something like this happens, you might want to write a letter to the company. A **business letter** is a formal written message that tells a person or company about a problem or concern you have.

A Business Letter

★ Describes a problem
★ Asks for help in solving the problem
★ Begins with a heading and an inside address that gives the name, title, and address of the person receiving the letter
★ Has a greeting and a body, or main part
★ Ends with a closing and the writer's name, or signature
★ Uses language that fits the purpose of the letter

Meet the Writer

I'm glad I took the time to write a business letter to the company. They took my letter seriously and even sent me a new game player!

Mallory Crane
Iowa

Think It Through

The first step in writing a business letter is to know why you are writing. You also need to know whom to write to and what you want them to do.

Brainstorming

Mallory knew exactly why she was writing. She bought a new video game player that didn't work. Have you ever had a similar experience?

Your Turn

Maybe you had a toy that broke right away, a game that was missing pieces, or a T-shirt that faded the first time it was washed. Make a list of problems you would write to a company about. Use the chart as a model.

THINGS I BOUGHT	PROBLEMS
1. video game	doesn't work
2. T-shirt	color faded
3. game	missing pieces

Select a Topic

Look at your chart and ask yourself some questions.

- Do I have a real complaint?
- Do I know whom to write to? If I don't know, how easy will it be to find out?
- What do I want the person or company to do?

Design a Plan

Before Mallory wrote her letter, she got the name and address of the person at the toy company who could help her. Then she made a plan so she would know exactly what to say.

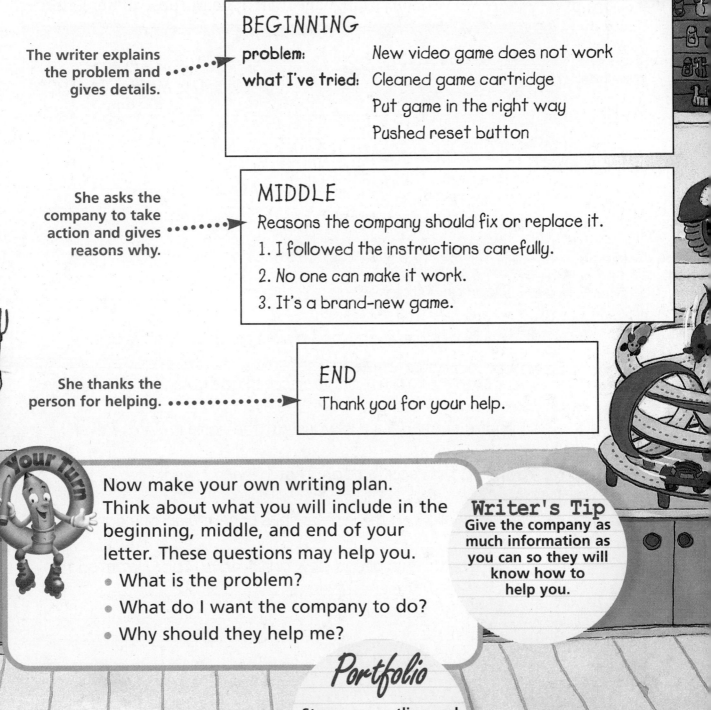

The writer explains the problem and gives details.

BEGINNING

problem: New video game does not work

what I've tried: Cleaned game cartridge

Put game in the right way

Pushed reset button

She asks the company to take action and gives reasons why.

MIDDLE

Reasons the company should fix or replace it.

1. I followed the instructions carefully.

2. No one can make it work.

3. It's a brand-new game.

She thanks the person for helping.

END

Thank you for your help.

Your Turn

Now make your own writing plan. Think about what you will include in the beginning, middle, and end of your letter. These questions may help you.

• What is the problem?

• What do I want the company to do?

• Why should they help me?

Writer's Tip
Give the company as much information as you can so they will know how to help you.

Portfolio

Store your outline and the company's name and address in your portfolio.

Put It Into Words

Mallory wanted her game player fixed. She wrote a letter to the store manager. Because she was writing a business letter, she was very polite. Does Mallory's language match the purpose of her letter?

The heading includes the writer's address and the date.

106 Sky Avenue
Des Moines, IA 50320
april 9, 1999

The inside address gives the name, title, and address of the person receiving the letter.

Mr. Ralph Kerman
Manager, Game Department
Tarzian Toys
1340 Thunder Lane
Chicago, Il 41456

The greeting is the opening of the letter. It ends with a colon (:).

Dear mr. Kerman:

The body is the main part of the letter.

   I bought a video game player and it doesn't work.

Whenever I turn it on, the screen goes blank. I cleaned the

game cartridges. I always put the game in right. I even

tryed the reset button. It still doesn't work.

   We followed the instructions carefully no one can get it

to work. It's a brand-new game, so my family wanted to

know if you could fix it?

   I hope you can help me.

The closing ends the letter.

Yours truly

The signature is the writer's name.

Mallory Crane

Think Like a Writer

As you begin your letter, ask yourself

★ **Subject:** What problem am I writing about?

★ **Audience:** Who can help me solve this problem?

★ **Purpose:** What do I want the company to do?

★ **Form:** What kind of language matches the purpose of my letter?

Mr. Kerman

Now you're ready to write the first draft of your letter. Be brief and businesslike.

- Start with a heading that gives your address and the date.

- Include an inside address with the name, title, and address of the person receiving the letter.

- Use *Dear* in the greeting. Use a colon (:) after the person's name.

- In the first paragraph, state the problem. Give details and tell what you've done.

- In the second paragraph, tell what you want the company or person to do about it and why.

- At the end, thank the person for helping.

- Use *Sincerely* or *Yours truly* in the closing. Then sign your name.

Conferencing

Read your letter to a partner. Ask if the problem is clearly described. Does the language match the kind of letter you're writing?

Writer's Tip
The tone of your letter should be polite, even if you are upset with the company.

Tech Tip
For a business letter, use plain type that's easy to read.

Portfolio
Save your drafts for the next step in the process, which is revising.

Take Another Look

Mallory felt her second paragraph—telling what she wanted the store to do—needed some work. She also realized she had forgotten to thank Mr. Kerman. Is there anything else she should add?

106 Sky Avenue
Des Moines, IA 50320
april 9, 1999

Mr. Ralph Kerman
Manager, Game Department
Tarzian Toys
1340 Thunder Lane
Chicago, Il 41456

Add an important detail.

Dear mr. Kerman:

on March 12, 1999,
I bought a video game player and it doesn't work.

Whenever I turn it on, the screen goes blank. I cleaned the

game cartridges. I always put the game in right. I even

tryed the reset button. It still doesn't work.

Correct a run-on sentence.

but
We followed the instructions carefully, no one can get it

to work. It's a brand-new game, so my family wanted to

Offer another way to solve the problem.

If not, can you return my money? Here is a copy of the sales slip.
know if you could fix it?

Thank the person for reading the letter.

Thank you for reading my letter.
I hope you can help me.

Yours truly

Mallory Crane

Read your business letter aloud. Put yourself in the position of the person receiving it. What else would this person want to know? When you make your changes, use the Revising Checklist as a guide.

Revising Marks

≡   capitalize
∧   add
✐   remove
⊙   add a period
／   make lowercase
◠   move
Ↄ   transpose

REVISING CHECKLIST

- Is the problem explained clearly?
- Have I given reasons for what I want done?
- Have I used the correct language for a business letter?
- Does the letter follow correct business letter form?
- Have I corrected any run-on sentences?

Conferencing

Ask a partner how you could improve your letter. Is the problem explained clearly? Did you give good reasons for what you want?

Writer's Tip

If you're polite, the person receiving the letter will be more likely to help you.

Portfolio

Save sales slips and other important papers in your portfolio, along with your drafts.

Become a Super Writer

Run-on sentences make your writing hard to understand. Try to avoid them. For help, see page 229 in the *Writer's Handbook* section.

Polish Your Writing

Mallory wanted her letter to look and sound right so the company would pay attention to her. She proofread it carefully. What do you think Mr. Kerman will think of her letter?

Capitalize the name of a month. ⟶

106 Sky Avenue
Des Moines, IA 50320
april 9, 1999

Mr. Ralph Kerman
Manager, Game Department
Tarzian Toys
1340 Thunder Lane
Capitalize the letters in the abbreviation of a state. ⟶ Chicago, Il 41456

Capitalize a person's title. ⟶ Dear mr. Kerman:

I bought a video game player on March 12, 1999, and it doesn't work. Whenever I turn it on, the screen goes blank.

I cleaned the game cartridges. I always put the game in
Correct a spelling mistake. ⟶ tried
right. I even (fryed) the reset button. It still doesn't work.

We followed the instructions carefully, but no one can get it to work. It's a brand-new game, so my family wanted to

Correct the punctuation mark at the end of a sentence. ⟶ know if you could fix it. If not, can you return my money?

Here is a copy of the sales slip.

Thank you for reading my letter. I hope you can help me.

Yours truly

Mallory Crane

Add a comma after the closing. ⟶

You're almost ready to mail (or maybe E-mail) your letter. As always, look your work over carefully for punctuation or spelling errors. Use the checklist.

¶	indent first line of paragraph
≡	capitalize
∧or∨	add
⌀	remove
⊙	add a period
/	make lowercase
◯	spelling mistake
◡	move
∾	transpose

Editing and Proofreading Checklist

- Did I capitalize proper names in all parts of the letter?
  See page 251 in the *Writer's Handbook* section.
- Did I use punctuation marks correctly?
  See pages 253–258 in the *Writer's Handbook* section.
- Did I spell words with endings correctly?
  See page 266 in the *Writer's Handbook* section.
- Is my handwriting neat and easy to read?
  See page 261 in the *Writer's Handbook* section.

Tech Tip
Use Print Preview to see how your letter will look when it's printed.

Conferencing

Ask a partner to double-check your work. Are all proper names and titles capitalized? Did you use commas correctly? Is your letter ready to send?

Portfolio
Save your notes, revisions, and final draft until you are ready to mail your letter.

Become a Super Writer

Be sure to capitalize letter and envelope parts correctly. For help, see page 251 in the *Writer's Handbook* section.

US MAIL

Share Your Work

Mallory printed her final copy on stationery. After the closing, she signed her name in her best handwriting and carefully folded the letter. Now what does she need to do?

106 Sky Avenue
Des Moines, IA 50320
April 9, 1999

Mr. Ralph Kerman
Manager, Game Department
Tarzian Toys
1340 Thunder Lane
Chicago, IL 41456

Dear Mr. Kerman:

I bought a video game player on March 12, 1999, and it doesn't work. Whenever I turn it on, the screen goes blank. I cleaned the game cartridges. I always put the game in right. I even tried the reset button. It still doesn't work.

We followed the instructions carefully, but no one can get it to work. It's a brand-new game, so my family wanted to know if you could fix it. If not, can you return my money? Here is a copy of the sales slip.

Thank you for reading my letter. I hope you can help me.

Yours truly,

Mallory Crane

Mallory Crane

Mallory Crane
106 Sky Avenue
Des Moines, IA 50320

Mr. Ralph Kerman
Manager, Game Department
Tarzian Toys
1340 Thunder Lane
Chicago, IL 41456

Mail Your Letter ▶

Now you're ready to address your envelope and seal your letter.

- Put the name, title, company name, and address of the person receiving the letter in the middle of the envelope.

- Put your name and address in the upper left-hand corner of the envelope.

- Put a stamp in the upper right-hand corner of the envelope.

◀ Award-Winning Letters

Make a display of business letters written by the class. Give the best letter the "Most Likely to Get Answered" award. As the letters are answered, display the replies next to the original letters.

Make Your Own ▶ Letterhead

Many companies use special stationery called **letterhead**. The name of the company, its address, and its phone number are printed at the top of each sheet of paper. Collect samples of letterhead. Then design letterhead for your class.

Martin Luther King Elementary School
Room 303
134 Tenth Avenue
Chicago, Illinois 46489
(529) 762-9812

Writing a Poster

What's a quick, colorful, eye-catching way to deliver a message? Look around—you'll see **posters** everywhere. A poster is a short written announcement, which usually has pictures. It tells about an event and encourages people to attend.

Meet the Writer

Doing something for the community is important. I made this poster to encourage people to recycle.

Tony Quintana
New Mexico

You CAN Do It! ◄········

DON'T throw your cans in the trash.

Recycle them. It's easy.

Come to the

RECYCLING RALLY

Saturday, March 22, at 10 A.M. ◄········

Lower School Playground

Save our resources.

Save the environment. ◄········

Talk About the Model

★ What first catches your eye on the poster?

★ Would this poster make you want to come to the Recycling Rally? Why or why not?

★ Why did the writer choose these pictures for his poster?

A clever title gets the reader's attention.

Information is clearly stated.

Reasons are given to persuade the reader.

Glass

Paper

Plastic

Aluminum

Make a Plan

Work by yourself or in a small group. Decide what event you want to make a poster for.

- Think about the information you need to include. Use the chart below.
- Decide how to illustrate your poster.

What event is it?

  The Recycling Rally

Why will people want to go?

  It's a good cause. People know they should recycle. It's good for the environment.

Who should go?

  Kids, families, teachers

When and where does it take place?

  March 22 at 10 A.M. at the playground

Write It Down

- Write a funny or clever title.
- Give all the important information about the event.
- Write short, snappy sentences.
- Give reasons why people should come.
- Add pictures or photographs.

Conferencing

Talk about your poster with a partner. Have you left out any important information? Does the poster convince your partner to attend?

Look It Over

Read your poster carefully. Correct any grammar or spelling mistakes.

WRITER'S HANDBOOK

WRITER'S
CRAFT

Alliteration is when two or more words in a sentence begin with the same consonant sound. Writers use alliteration to make words fun to read.

In this sentence, the writer repeats the sound of *h*.

A herd of horses headed into the hills.

In a poem or a story, you can use alliteration to make your writing more interesting. Your readers will enjoy the rhythm and the repeated sounds.

▶ **For help with rhythm, see page 220.**

Remember:
Repetition and rhythm keep readers reading.

A **character** is a person in a story. It can also be an animal who acts like a person. Writers try to make their characters act like real people. They show what characters think and feel and how they look and act.

Habib looks like a shy little kid. But when he puts on a pair of skates—watch out! He zooms down the sidewalk, zigzagging around people and over bumps. He skates in circles around his friends. When they race, he always wins. Habib is the best skater in the school.

When you write, look for ways to make your characters real.

Details

Details create a picture for the reader. Writers use them to make stories seem real. They also use details to support their main ideas.

Sensory Words

Sensory words describe what people see, hear, touch, smell, taste, and feel.

> An apple is my favorite fruit. I like its red, shiny color. I like to feel its smooth skin in my hand. I like the crunch it makes when I bite it. The best part is the sweet juice that runs down my chin.

Sensory words make poems and stories come alive.

Examples

Examples are facts that writers use to support their ideas and opinions.

opinion: Everyone should know how to swim.

examples: Swimming is good exercise.
Swimming keeps you cool in the summer.
Swimming could someday save your life.

You have to give your readers good reasons to agree with you. List all the reasons you feel the way you do and then choose the ones that are most important.

Remember:
Good examples should really prove your point.

Dialogue is a conversation between two or more people in a story. When characters speak, they tell readers what they are thinking and feeling.

In the example, Toby's words tell how much she wants to go to the beach and how excited she is when her grandfather says he'll take her.

> "Can we go to the beach today?" Toby asked hopefully.
>
> "Your father needs the car today," Mom replied.
>
> "Well, can't we take the bus? Please, I really want to go," Toby pleaded.
>
> "The bus takes too long," said Mom.
>
> "I'll ask Grandpa. Maybe he'll take me. I love making sand castles with him!"
>
> Toby dashed out of the room. She was back in a few minutes, with a big smile on her face.
>
> "Grandpa's going to take us to the beach!" she exclaimed. "Hurry up, let's get ready!"

When you write dialogue, use quotation marks. Put them at the beginning and end of the speaker's exact words.

▶ **For help with quotation marks, see page 260.**

Remember:
Dialogue helps the reader get to know the characters.

Exaggeration

Exaggeration is the use of words to make something seem bigger, stronger, sillier, or smarter than it really is. Writers often exaggerate to make a point or when they write humorous stories.

My dog is so famous he gets birthday cards from the President of the United States.

My brother loves to eat. Yesterday he had 50 hamburgers, 30 hot dogs, and 10 pounds of French fries—and that was just for lunch!

Exaggeration is a way of describing a character that also makes your writing fun to read.

Humor

Remember:

Humor makes your writing more fun.

Humor is what makes people laugh. Often the funniest things come from everyday experiences.

I woke up late one day. The school bus was almost at the door. I didn't even have time to turn on the light. I pulled on my clothes, grabbed two shoes off the closet floor, and flew out the front door.

When I got on the bus, everyone began laughing. I couldn't figure out why. Then I looked down at my feet. On my left foot, I was wearing a purple shoe. On my right foot, I was wearing a brown one!

When you use humor in your writing, think about your audience. What would make them laugh?

Language is the spoken or written words people use to tell their thoughts and feelings. Writers choose their words carefully. The language they use matches their purpose and audience.

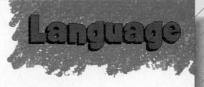

Formal Language

Alex needs to write a thank-you note to the store owner who sponsors her soccer team. She is writing to an adult for an official reason, so she uses **formal language**.

Dear Mr. Stanton,

   Thank you for the T-shirts you gave our team. The new team emblem on the front looks wonderful. We will proudly wear our T-shirts at every game.

                    Sincerely,
                    Alex Martin

Informal Language

In a letter to a friend, the writer would use **informal language**. It fits the purpose of a friendly letter.

Dear Maria,

   Guess what! We won every game this season. And we got these really cool T-shirts for our team! Wish I could send you one. Write soon.

                    Your friend,
                    Alex

Before you begin to write, think about your purpose and audience. Ask yourself, why am I writing this? Who will be reading it?

Remember:
Keep your purpose and audience in mind while you are writing.

Metaphor

A **metaphor** is a comparison. It suggests that two different things are alike in some ways.

His mind is a closed door.

The cold wind was a slap in the face.

Writers use metaphors to make the reader see something familiar in a new and special way. Metaphors work well in poems and stories.

A **simile** is another kind of comparison. It uses *like* or *as* to make a comparison.

▶ **For help with similes, see page 222.**

Onomatopoeia

Whoosh, clang, hiss, buzz, and *snap* are all examples of **onomatopoeia**. Onomatopoeia is the use of words that sound like their meanings.

In the first example, the word *thump* actually sounds like something is hitting the floor. In the second example, the word *whoosh* sounds like the noise made by something moving very fast.

Thump, thump, thump goes my dog's tail. Her new chew toy makes her very happy.

Whoosh! The train went by so fast I almost didn't see it.

In stories and poems, onomatopoeia lets readers actually hear what's happening.

Remember:
Sound effects make your writing fun to read.

Writers want to present their ideas in ways that are clear and easy to follow. Time order, space order, and order of importance are three ways writers organize information.

Order of Ideas and Events

Time order is the order in which events happen in real life. In a story, a writer often tells what happened *first,* then *next,* then *last.* These words let the reader know when each event took place.

> We were hungry, so we ate lunch first. Next, we played baseball. Last, we went for a swim to cool off.

Writers often use **space order** to describe what something looks like. Something can be described from the top to the bottom, from the front to the back, or from left to right. Words like *in front of* and *behind* help describe the space order of things.

> At the front of the train was a huge black engine. Behind it were boxcars and a caboose.

Order of importance is another way to organize writing. The most important ideas come first. The less important ideas come next.

> Who can resist pancakes for breakfast? They give you energy. They taste great. They're very filling, so you won't get hungry before lunch. Pancakes make a good breakfast.

Remember:
When you write, think about the best order to present your ideas.

All good writing needs a clear beginning, middle, and end.

Beginning

The **beginning** should catch the reader's interest. In a story, the plot and characters are often introduced in the beginning.

> Have you ever lived through a tornado? I did. Scared doesn't begin to tell you how I felt.

In other kinds of writing, you can start with a topic sentence. It tells readers what you're writing about.

Middle

In a story, the **middle** gives the main events.

> The sky turned dark and angry. The wind picked up, and it began to rain. In the distance I heard a roar like a train. It was coming closer. We ran down the basement steps and bolted the door just in time.

In other kinds of writing, the middle gives examples and supporting details.

End

The **end** tells what happens.

> Suddenly, everything was quiet again. We came out of the basement and looked around. The sun was out, and the sky was calm. There was no sign of the tornado.

In other kinds of writing, the end sums up your main ideas.

Personification makes something that is not human seem like a person.

> At night the flowers go to sleep.
>
> The dog looked sad when we left.
>
> The sun smiled in the sky.

Personification helps create a picture in the reader's mind. Use personification when you write stories and poems.

Remember:
Personification is a good way to describe something.

The **plot** is what happens in a story. Writers make sure that the action in a plot keeps readers interested.

Beginning

In the **beginning**, the characters and setting are introduced. Sometimes the writer starts off with an important event or a problem to solve.

Middle

In the **middle**, the writer builds suspense to keep the reader interested. The action moves toward a high point of excitement.

> The soccer team wins a tough game.
>
> Maria finds her lost dog.
>
> Mike's friends jump up and yell, "Surprise!"

End

The **end** tells how everything turns out. When you write a story, decide what the high point will be. Then think of events that lead up to that high point. Make them seem as real as you can.

Point of View

The **point of view** tells whether the writer is talking about a personal experience or something that happened to someone else.

First Person

If the story is written in the **first person**, the writer is telling about a personal experience. The writer uses the words *I*, *me*, and *my* to tell what happens to the main character.

> My father drives a truck. It's a 16 wheeler. Last summer, I rode with Dad on a cross-country trip. I brought my camera with me so that I could take pictures of the places we visited. We drove through ten different states.

Third Person

If the story is written in the **third person**, the writer is telling about someone else. The writer uses words such as *he, she,* and *they* to tell what happened to the main character.

> Pam and Todd were both trying out for the school play. Pam went first. She had read the part over and over again until she knew the lines by heart. Todd went next. He was perfect for the role. In the end, they both got the parts they wanted.

As you plan a story, decide which point of view you will use.

▶ **For help with pronouns, see pages 244–246.**

Remember:
Don't change your point of view in the middle of a story.

In a story, the **problem** is what the main character must solve. It can be a problem between two people, something that happens to a character, or a decision a character must make.

> Myra is always picking on Amy.
>
> Greg hears a grizzly bear outside his tent.
>
> Both of Sandy's friends want her on their soccer teams.

When you plan your story, first decide on the problem and then think of the different ways your character might solve it.

Problem

Remember:
Choose a problem that your readers will understand.

The biggest challenge for a writer is to keep the readers interested. The writer has to get the readers' attention and then keep them reading to the end.

Reader Interest

Title

An interesting **title** gets readers' attention. The title should not give away the plot.

> Frog on the Loose!

Beginning

A strong **beginning** makes readers want to keep reading.

> My frog can jump really high. One day he jumped out of his tank.

End

A strong **end** makes readers glad they finished the story.

> That crazy frog stayed hidden for three whole days until we found him.

Rhyme

When writers use **rhyme**, they repeat similar sounds at the ends of words. Many poems have words at the end of each line that rhyme.

In the example, the first two lines and the second two lines of the poem rhyme.

> Did you read this book?
> Come and take a look.
> It's about a strange old house
> And the owner, who's a mouse.

When you write a rhyming poem, first make a list of words that rhyme.

Rhythm

Rhythm is the pattern that sounds make. In many poems and songs, the rhythm follows a regular pattern.

In this familiar nursery rhyme, it's easy to find the pattern in the sounds.

> Jack and Jill went up the hill
> To fetch a pail of water.
> Jack fell down and broke his crown,
> And Jill came tumbling after.

When you are writing a rhyme or poem, try to make a rhythm that will form a musical pattern.

Experienced writers change the beginnings, the lengths, and the kinds of sentences they use to keep their writing interesting.

Variety

Writers use all types of sentences. Some sentences tell things. Some ask questions or give commands. The mix of sentences keeps the writing interesting.

> Stop. What's that sound? It must be a siren. The fire truck is coming!

Length

Writers also mix short sentences with long sentences. They don't want every sentence to sound the same.

> The circus came to town yesterday. When we entered the big top, the first thing we saw were the clowns. They were great!

One way to make longer sentences is to combine short ones.

> We got up. We walked the dog. We left for school.
>
> We got up, walked the dog, and left for school.

▶ **For help combining sentences, see pages 229 and 247.**

Remember: There are many ways to make your sentences interesting.

Beginnings

Writing can become boring when all the sentences begin the same way. By changing the words that begin each sentence, writers keep their readers' attention.

> I was climbing a rock when my foot slipped. As I started to fall, I grabbed a small branch. "Help!" I shouted at the top of my voice.

Setting

The **setting** is when and where a story takes place. Writers often describe the setting at the very start of the story.

> It was the first day of spring. Hundreds of bikes filled the roads of Tabor Park. The biggest bike race of the year was about to begin.

You can make the setting anywhere you like—a beach, a playground, a spooky old house, or somewhere in a make-believe world. It's your choice. Give readers details to make the setting seem real.

▶ **For help with details and descriptive words, see pages 210 and 224.**

Simile

A **simile** is a comparison. It uses the words *like* or *as* to show that two things are alike in some way. Writers use similes in stories and poems.

> The skater is as graceful as a bird in flight.
> The black panther moved like a shadow in the night.

Similes make readers see something familiar in a new way.

A metaphor also compares two different things, but it does not use the words *like* or *as*.

▶ **For help with metaphors, see page 214.**

Remember:
Always use *like* or *as* when you write a simile.

Voice is the way writers express ideas. Different voices are used for different kinds of writing.

Lyric Voice

A **lyric voice** is a poet's voice. It lets a writer focus on feelings and descriptions.

> Today is a very gray day.
> My best friend has moved away.

Remember: Let your writing sound as if it comes from your heart.

You use a lyric voice when you write a poem. You also use it when you want to paint a picture with words.

Narrative Voice

A **narrative voice** is a storyteller's voice. It can be serious, funny, or even mysterious. Sometimes the writer tells a story about other people, and sometimes the writer is the main character.

> How did I know that visiting my cousins was going to get me into trouble? It all started when we played hide-and-seek. We ran into the woods behind their house. I got lost.

Remember to use *I* and *me* when you write about yourself, and *he, she* and *they* when you write about someone else.

> Tanya wanted to play softball on her school team more than anything else. Every afternoon, her cousin practiced with her. They played catch. He pitched, and she practiced batting. Finally, the day of tryouts came. Tanya knew she was ready.

▶ **For help with pronouns, see pages 244–246.**

Words

Writers are always looking for the best word to tell about something. When you revise your writing, look for words that don't tell enough. These are words you could replace with better words.

Precise Words

Writers try to use **precise words** to say exactly what they mean. Precise words are more interesting. They give the reader a better understanding of what the writer is trying to say.

> Kevin spun around and grabbed the ball. He sprinted down the court, the ball pounding in front of him. The net was clear. He held his breath, crouched, and sprang. Swish! The ball sailed through the hoop.

Descriptive Words

Descriptive words show readers how things look, sound, taste, smell, and feel.

> My closet is a nightmare. It smells like a locker room. Shoes, clothes, and toys are piled on the floor. Somewhere in the mess my lost watch glows in the dark and beeps every hour. Tangled coat hangers jab my hand like sharp teeth. A monster may even be in there somewhere!

A thesaurus can help you find the right words.

▶ For help in using a thesaurus, see page 275.

▶ For help with sensory words, see page 210.

GRAMMAR, USAGE, MECHANICS, SPELLING

A **sentence** is a group of words that expresses a complete thought. A sentence has two parts: the subject and the predicate.

Subject

The **complete subject** includes all the words that tell who or what is doing something.

Nicholas rode his new bike.

His friend Jake has a new bike, too.

The **simple subject** is the main word in a complete subject.

The pitcher threw a curve ball.

The batter hit the ball to third base.

Predicate

The **complete predicate** tells what action the subject does or what the subject is like.

Nicholas sped down the road.

His new bike is green and yellow.

The **simple predicate** is the main word in the complete predicate.

The catcher threw the ball to the pitcher.

The batter ran to second base.

Remember:
A sentence has a subject and a predicate and expresses a complete thought.

Every sentence has a subject and a predicate. Some sentences have two subjects. This is a **compound subject**. Some sentences have two predicates. This is a **compound predicate**.

★ **Simple Sentences**

A **simple sentence** has one complete thought. It may have more than one subject and predicate.

one subject and one predicate:	The waves tumbled.
compound subject:	Whales **and** dolphins **swam.**
compound predicate:	Flying fish leaped **and** soared.
two subjects and two predicates:	Tim **and** I watched **and** shouted.

> **Remember:**
> A compound sentence is two simple sentences joined together.

★ **Compound Sentences**

A **compound sentence** is made up of two or more simple sentences. The sentences usually are joined by a comma (,) and the words *and, but, or, for, nor, so,* or *yet*.

The sky grew dark, and the rain poured down.

I walked outside, but I didn't have an umbrella.

I can go without an umbrella, or I can stay home.

Soon the rain stopped, and the sun came out.

Word Order

A sentence in **natural word order** has the subject first, followed by the predicate.

> subject predicate
>
> The children ran into the playground.

In some sentences the word order is changed. The predicate comes *before* the subject.

In a question the predicate comes before the subject.

> predicate subject
>
> Where are the toys?

When a sentence begins with *here* or *there*, the predicate comes before the subject.

> predicate subject
>
> Here are the red brick houses.

Sometimes writers change the word order to make sentences sound different from one another.

> A big dog leaped over the fence.
>
> Over the fence leaped a big dog.

Sentence Fragments

A **sentence fragment** is a sentence that is not complete. It is missing either a subject or a predicate. A fragment does not make sense because it is not a complete thought.

> fragment: The whole class
>
> complete sentence: The whole class went to
>   the museum.

A **run-on sentence** is two complete sentences that run together. It is missing punctuation or a connecting word such as *and, but*, or *or*.

A run-on sentence can be corrected by making two separate sentences or by adding a comma and a connecting word.

run-on sentence:	The sun appeared the birds chirped.
two sentences:	The sun appeared. The birds chirped.
run-on sentence:	I saw the movie I didn't like it.
combined sentence:	I saw the movie, but I didn't like it.

Writers try to avoid using too many short, choppy sentences. Often, two short sentences or sentence parts can be **combined** with a connecting word.

short sentences:	We went to the zoo. We looked at the lions. We visited the polar bears.
combined:	We went to the zoo. We looked at the lions, and we visited the polar bears.

Remember:
Use a variety of sentences to keep your writing interesting.

Sometimes writers add information to **expand** sentences and make them more interesting.

We went to the zoo on Saturday. First, we looked at the lions sleeping under a tree. Then, we visited the huge white polar bears.

There are four kinds of sentences. Each kind has a different purpose.

★ Declarative Sentences

A **declarative sentence** tells something. It ends with a period (.).

> The capital of Texas is Austin.

★ Interrogative Sentences

An **interrogative sentence** asks a question. It ends with a question mark (?).

> What is the tallest building in Dallas?

★ Imperative Sentences

An **imperative sentence** tells someone to do something. It ends with a period (.).

> Wear a seat belt in a car.

The subject of an imperative sentence is not always directly stated. Sometimes the subject *you* is simply understood to be part of the sentence.

> (You) Never speak with strangers.

★ Exclamatory Sentences

An **exclamatory sentence** shows strong feeling or surprise. It ends with an exclamation point (!).

> There's a lion in the backyard!

Remember:
Complete sentences have subjects and predicates and a punctuation mark at the end.

A **noun** is a word that names a person, place, or thing.

people	teacher	brother	friend	painter
places	park	kitchen	city	classroom
things	shoe	machine	egg	dinosaur

Common Nouns

A **common noun** is the general name of a person, place, or thing. Common nouns are not capitalized.

woman   state   car

Proper Nouns

A **proper noun** is the name of a specific person, place, or thing. Proper nouns are always capitalized.

Beverly Cleary   Kansas   Liberty Bell

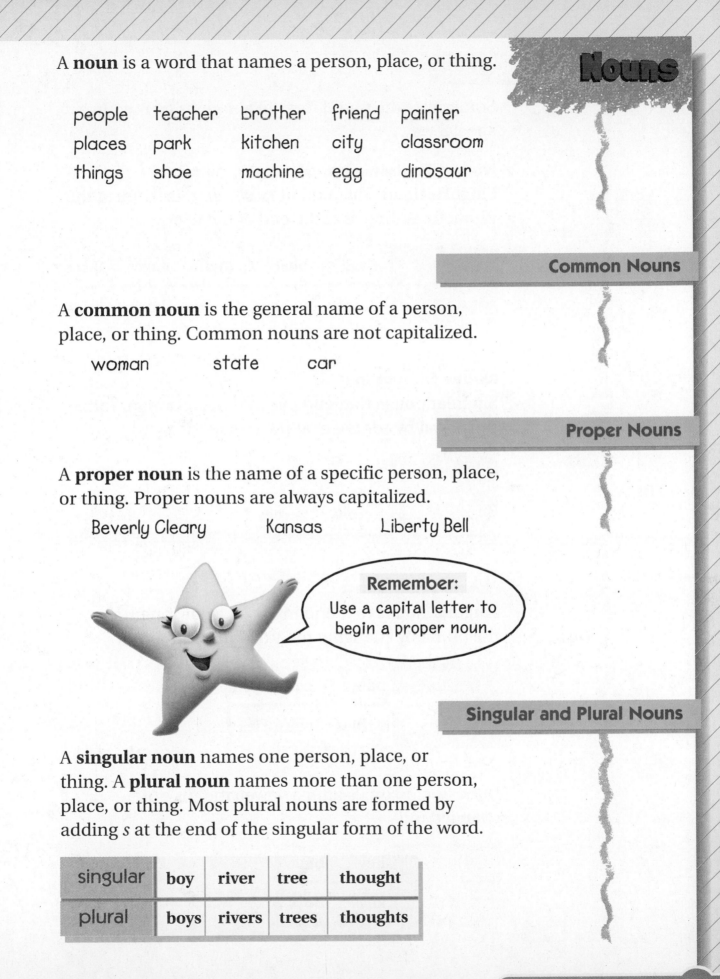

Remember:
Use a capital letter to begin a proper noun.

Singular and Plural Nouns

A **singular noun** names one person, place, or thing. A **plural noun** names more than one person, place, or thing. Most plural nouns are formed by adding *s* at the end of the singular form of the word.

singular	boy	river	tree	thought
plural	boys	rivers	trees	thoughts

Irregular Plural Nouns

Sometimes the plural form of a noun is formed in a special way.

★ **Nouns Ending in *ss*, *sh*, *ch*, *x*, or *zz***

Singular nouns that end in *ss, sh, ch, x,* or *zz* form the plural by adding *es* at the end of the word.

singular	glass	bush	inch	box	buzz
plural	glasses	bushes	inches	boxes	buzzes

★ **Nouns Ending in *o***

Singular nouns that end in *o* after a consonant form the plural by adding *es* at the end of the word.

singular	hero	zero
plural	heroes	zeroes

★ **Nouns Ending in *y***

Singular nouns that end in *y* after a consonant form the plural by changing the *y* to *i* and adding *es*.

singular	baby	country
plural	babies	countries

If the final *y* comes after a vowel, the *y* is not changed to *i*.

singular	key	boy
plural	keys	boys

★ Nouns With Special Plural Forms

Some nouns have special plural forms.

singular	child	goose	mouse
plural	children	geese	mice

A **possessive noun** shows that someone or something owns something.

The possessive form of most singular nouns is formed by adding *'s* at the end of the word.

> Jamal lost Jack's favorite cap.

The possessive form of a plural noun ending in *s* is formed by adding an apostrophe (').

> Chris looked for the cap in the boys' locker room.

The possessive form of a plural noun with a special spelling is formed by adding *'s*.

> Jamal found a new one in a children's store.

Remember:
Possessive nouns always have an apostrophe (').

Verbs

Every sentence must have a **verb**. The verb is the main word or words in the predicate of a sentence.

Action Verbs

An **action verb** tells what the subject of a sentence does or did.

> We play soccer every Saturday morning.
>
> I kicked the ball with my feet.

Helping Verbs

A **helping verb** comes before the main verb. It helps the main verb show when something happened.

> Julie is helping us learn the game.
>
> Did she help you?
>
> Julie has coached the team for two years.
>
> Julie will coach our team next year.

Common Helping Verbs				
am	are	been	can	could
did	do	had	has	have
is	may	might	must	shall
should	was	were	will	would

Remember:
Use helping verbs to help action verbs show time.

A **linking verb** does not show action. It connects the subject of the sentence to a noun or describing word.

noun:　　Those neighbors are our friends.

describing word:　　Their dog is small and fluffy.

Different forms of the verb *be* are linking verbs. The ones used most often are *am, are, were, is,* and *was.*

I am a third grader.

You are a third grader, too.

We were in second grade last year.

She is in fourth grade now.

I was the youngest one in my class.

Other Linking Verbs

There are several **other linking verbs** besides *be.* These verbs usually tell what things are like or what they will become.

It looks as if it's going to rain.

The sky seems very dark.

The wind feels stronger, too.

Linking Verbs

appear	become	feel	look
seem	smell	sound	taste

Remember:
Linking verbs do not show action.

Tense tells when the action of a verb takes place. When you write, you show the tense of a verb by adding endings or by using a helping verb.

★ **Present Tense**

The **present tense** tells about an action that is happening now. It can also state an action that happens regularly.

> The mayor speaks to the crowd.
>
> He gives a speech every Fourth of July.
>
> He is speaking right now.

★ **Past Tense**

A verb in the **past tense** tells about an action that happened some time ago.

> We liked the mayor's speech.
>
> Last year, he spoke too long.

When you write, be careful not to use different tenses in the same sentence or in nearby sentences.

> incorrect: We go to the beach often.
>   We enjoyed it a lot.
>
> correct: We go to the beach often.
>   We enjoy it a lot.

★ **Future Tense**

The **future tense** tells about an action that has not yet happened. It will happen sometime in the future.

> Tomorrow, I will start my science project.
>
> My teacher will help me after school on Wednesday.
>
> The science fair will take place next month.

The **subject** and **verb** in a sentence must agree in number. If the subject is singular, the verb must be singular, too.

Matt likes computer games.

He plays them often.

If the subject is plural, the verb must be plural, too.

My friends like these games, too.

They play often.

Most verbs are **regular verbs**. To use these verbs to tell about an action in the past, add *ed*.

present tense: They talk.

I laugh.

She listens.

past tense: They talked.

I laughed.

She listened.

A helping verb can also be used with *ed* to tell about an action that happened in the past.

They talked. They have talked. They had talked.

Remember:
To form the past tense, add *ed* to regular verbs.

Some verbs are not regular. For **irregular verbs**, you do not add *ed* to tell about an action in the past. Instead, you form the past tense in special ways.

present tense: The birds fly over our house.

past tense: The birds flew over our house.

present tense: The play begins at eight o'clock.

past tense: The play began at eight o'clock.

past tense with
helping verb: The play has begun already.

Remember:
To check whether a verb is regular or irregular, look up the word in a dictionary.

Here are the present, past, and helping-verb forms of some common irregular verbs.

Present Tense	Past Tense	Past With Helping Verbs
begin	began	has/had begun
bring	brought	has/had brought
come	came	has/had come
eat	ate	has/had eaten
give	gave	has/had given
go	went	has/had gone
let	let	has/had let
ring	rang	has/had rung
run	ran	has/had run
see	saw	has/had seen
sing	sang	has/had sung
sleep	slept	has/had slept
take	took	has/had taken

Some **verbs** cause problems if they are not used carefully.

★ **May/Can**

May is used to ask permission.
Can shows that someone is able to do something.

> May I borrow your book?

> I can finish it by tomorrow.

★ **Sit/Set**

Sit means "to rest or stay in one place."
Set means "to put."

> My uncle sits on the porch every evening.

> Set that package on the table, please.

★ **Let/Leave**

Let means "to allow."
Leave means "to go away" or "to let be."

> Mom let me hold the new baby.

> I have to leave for school at seven o'clock.

> Please leave the computer on when you finish.

Remember:
If you're not sure what a verb means, look it up in the dictionary.

★ **Lie/Lay**

Lie means "to stretch oneself out in a flat position."
Lay is the past tense of *lie*. It also means "to put something down."

> The cat likes to lie in the sun.

> She lay in the window until it got dark.

> Lay the box gently on the floor.

★ **Rise/Raise**

Rise means "to get up." **Raise** means "to lift up."

> The sun rises in the east.

> Dan raised the window to let some air in.

Adjectives

An **adjective** is a word that describes a noun. An adjective gives important details. It helps express ideas more clearly.

Adjectives are words that describe people, places, and things.

Five kittens slept in the little basket.

They had pink noses and soft fur.

Adjectives usually tell *what kind, which one,* or *how many.*

what kind:	bright lights	red apples
which one:	first base	each number
how many:	one box	all horses

Articles

The words *a, an,* and *the* are special adjectives called **articles**.

A rose is a flower.

I ate an apple and an orange for dessert.

We invited the other class on the trip.

Use *a* with nouns that begin with the sound of a consonant.
Use *an* with nouns that begin with a vowel.

a	an
a nest	an egg
a plum	an apple
a boat	an island
a fish	an otter
a raindrop	an umbrella

Adjectives can be used to compare people, places, and things.

> Randy is younger than his sister.

> Sam's sneakers are bigger than mine.

A **comparative adjective** compares two things. Add *er* to an adjective with one syllable, or use the word *more* before an adjective of two or more syllables.

> This dog is older than our puppy.

> That puppy is more playful than our dog.

A **superlative adjective** compares more than two things. Add *est* to an adjective with one syllable, or use the word *most* before an adjective of two or more syllables.

> Alan is the oldest of three children.

> He is the most athletic as well.

The adjective **good** has special forms.

Better is the comparative form. Use **better** to compare two people or things.

Best is the superlative form. Use **best** to compare three or more people or things.

> A turkey sandwich is good.

> A turkey sandwich with cheese is better.

> A turkey sandwich with cheese, lettuce, and tomato is the best.

Remember:
Never use the words *more* or *most* with adjectives ending in *er* or *est*.

Adverbs

An **adverb** is a word that describes a verb, an adjective, or another adverb. Adverbs should be placed near the words they tell about.

describes a verb:	The baby crawls slowly.
describes an adjective:	The music was quite slow.
describes an adverb:	The turtle crawled very slowly.

Most adverbs answer the questions *where, when,* or *how.*

where:	The cow lives here on our farm.
when:	We awaken early in the morning.
how:	The goats ate quickly.

Using Adverbs Correctly

Sometimes adverbs and adjectives are similar. These are a few that are easy to confuse.

★ **Real/Very**

Real is an adjective, and **very** is an adverb. **Real** cannot be used to mean "very."

These are real flowers in the vase.

It is very hot today.

★ **Good/Well**

Good is an adjective, and **well** is an adverb.

Inez is a good runner.

Inez runs well.

Remember:
Most adverbs tell *where, how,* or *when.*

Like adjectives, adverbs can be used to compare. A **comparative adverb** compares two actions. Add **er** to short adverbs, and use **more** with adverbs that end with **ly**.

A **superlative adverb** compares three or more actions. Add **est** to short adverbs, and use **most** with adverbs that end with **ly**.

> Kisha *jumped* higher than Patty.
>
> She *jumped* highest of all.

> Joey reads more slowly than I do.
>
> Kate reads the most easily of all.

Remember:
Never use more than one negative In a sentence.

Negatives are words that mean "no."

> We will not ride bikes to school today.
>
> Pablo never rides his bike to school.

common negatives	no	not	never
	none	neither	

Use only one negative in each sentence.

> incorrect: I never **said** no such thing.
>
> correct: I never **said** any such thing.

Pronouns

A **pronoun** is a word that takes the place of a noun. Pronouns are used in different ways. Some replace the subject or object of a sentence. Others refer to people or show that something belongs to someone.

Personal Pronouns

Personal pronouns take the place of a noun or nouns in a sentence. Words such as *I* and *me* are personal pronouns.

nouns naming people: Tanya **invited the** girls.

personal pronouns: She **invited** them.

Pronouns must agree in number with the nouns they replace. Singular pronouns replace singular nouns. Plural pronouns replace plural nouns.

singular nouns: Peter **played catch with** Julie.

singular pronouns: He **played catch with** her.

plural nouns: The girls **raced the** boys.

plural pronouns: They **beat** them **in a race.**

singular	I, me	.you	he, she, it, him, her
plural	we, us	you	they, them

Subject Pronouns

A **subject pronoun** takes the place of a noun in the subject part of a sentence.

noun: Mike **painted a picture.**

subject pronoun: He **painted a picture.**

noun: The children **wrote a song.**

subject pronoun: They **wrote a song.**

singular	I	you	he, she, it
plural	we	you	they

An **object pronoun** takes the place of a noun that comes after an action verb. Object pronouns are used after words like *to, for, in, at, by, of,* and *with.*

noun: Ted gave Tamara a pencil.

object pronoun: Ted gave her a pencil.

noun: Priah walked home with Dina.

object pronoun: Priah walked home with her.

Remember:
Never use the word *I* after words such as *between, with, for,* or *to.*

singular	me	you	him, her, it
plural	us	you	them

Using I and Me

The word ***I*** is used as a subject pronoun. The word ***me*** is used as an object pronoun.

I visited *my* uncle last week.

I took the train from the city.

My uncle met me at the station.

He had a surprise for me.

Demonstrative Pronouns

A **demonstrative pronoun** points out a person or thing. It takes the place of a noun in a sentence. Use *this* and *these* to point out something nearby. Use *that* and *those* to point out something at a distance.

This is *my* bicycle here.

These are *my* sneakers next to it.

That is *our* car at the end of the row.

Those are *my* parents up ahead.

Pronouns

Possessive Pronouns

A **possessive pronoun** shows ownership. It is often used to describe a noun.

> My book bag will hold more than your bag.

singular	my	your	his, hers, its
plural	our	your	their

A possessive pronoun can be used alone, without a noun.

> The best story was yours.

> The idea for that story was mine.

singular	mine	yours	his, hers, its
plural	ours	yours	theirs

Agreement of Pronouns

Remember:
A pronoun must agree with the noun it replaces.

A pronoun agrees in number with the noun it replaces. A singular pronoun replaces a singular noun. A plural pronoun replaces a plural noun.

The pronouns *his* and *him* are used for men and boys. The pronouns *her* and *hers* are used for women and girls.

singular: Ben lent me his bike.
Sarah sang her song at the concert.

plural: The birds were building their nests.

A **preposition** is a word that shows how a noun or a pronoun relates to another word in the sentence.

> Lara and Kate spoke on the phone for an hour.

Common Prepositions			
at	by	down	from
in	of	on	over
through	to	up	with

Prepositional Phrases

A **prepositional phrase** is made up of a preposition and the words that go with it.

> Kate called with a question.
> We walked down the road.

A **conjunction** is a word that connects words or groups of words.

> The fans jumped and cheered.
> Sandy wants a bike or skates.

Coordinating conjunctions connect two or more words, phrases, or sentences.

> The sky was gray, and the wind blew.
> John loves ice cream, but not for breakfast.

Conjunctions						
and	or	but	nor	for	so	yet

Remember:
Use a conjunction to connect two or more words or phrases.

Capitalization

Capital letters are signals that tell readers what is to come. They also identify special people, places, and things.

First Word of a Sentence

The **first word of a sentence** always begins with a capital letter.

The food tastes great.

Please pass the potatoes.

Did you eat all the banana cake?

Pronoun *I*

Remember:

You are important. Always use a capital letter when you write the pronoun *I*.

The **pronoun *I*** is always capitalized.

I wiped the dishes.

My brother and I played ball later.

May I watch a video now?

Proper Nouns

Words used as **names** begin with a capital letter.

The phone call was for Dad.

Dan Richardson called from New Jersey.

The Red Cross needs old blankets.

A **title** used with someone's name begins with a capital letter.

Remember:
When you become president, don't forget to capitalize the first letter of your title.

President Lincoln

Queen Elizabeth II

General Washington

Initials are the first letters of a person's name. They are written with capital letters.

C. S. Lewis

J. F. K.

Robert E. Lee

An **abbreviation** is a short form of a word. Most abbreviations begin with a capital letter and end with a period.

Mr. Cutler

Dr. Seuss

Martin Luther King, Jr.

U.S.

The postal abbreviation for the name of a state has two letters. Both letters are capitalized.

New York	NY	Oregon	OR
Louisiana	LA	Texas	TX
West Virginia	WV	Maine	ME

Capitalization

Titles of Works and Headlines

Titles of books, poems, stories, magazines, songs, and movies are capitalized. The first, last, and all other important words in a title begin with a capital letter. Do not capitalize words like *the, an, in*, or *to* unless they are the first or last words.

book:	The Emperor and the Kite
magazine:	Highlights for Children
song:	"Twinkle, Twinkle, Little Star"
movie:	The Lion King

A **headline** is the title of a newspaper or magazine article. Use a capital letter to begin the first, last, and all other important words in a headline.

Yankees to Play in the World Series!

Third Grader Wins Writing Award

Snow Closes Schools for a Week

Geographical Names

Use a capital letter to begin specific **geographical** or **place names.** Geographical names include the names of particular cities, states, and countries. They also include bodies of water, planets, and other special places.

city:	San Antonio
state:	California
country:	South Africa
body of water:	Pacific Ocean
planet:	Jupiter
special place:	Grand Canyon

In the **heading** of a letter, begin the names of a street, city, state, and month with a capital letter.

heading: 346 Greenview Drive
            Grand Prairie, Texas 75050
            May 10, 2000

Use a capital letter to begin the first word in the **greeting** and **closing** of a letter. Remember to begin proper names and titles with capital letters.

greeting: Dear Aunt Helen,

closings: Sincerely,
             Sincerely yours,

Remember:
If I told you my name, you'd have to begin it with a capital letter.

Use a capital letter to begin the names of the **days** of the week, **months** of the year, and **holidays**.

In 2003, Independence Day will be Friday, July 4.

An **outline** is a plan for writing. An outline begins with a title. Use a Roman numeral and a period for a **main topic.** Use a capital letter and a period for a **subtopic.** Begin the first word of the main topic and the subtopic with a capital letter.

main topic: I. What Benjamin Banneker did
fact: A. Helped plan Washington, D.C.
fact: B. Wrote almanacs

A **quotation** is a person's exact words. In a story it tells what a character says.

Begin the first word of a direct quotation with a capital letter. A quotation can come before or after the rest of the sentence.

> Lucy said, "There is no heat in the house."

> "Our heater is broken," answered her mother.

There is a difference between a direct quotation and repeating what someone said.

direct quotation:	Mom said, "Wear a sweater."
not a quotation:	Mom said that I should wear a sweater.
direct quotation:	"I'm still cold," Lucy complained.
not a quotation:	Lucy complained that she was still cold.

▶ For help with quotation marks, see page 260.

Remember:
Always put quotation marks around a speaker's exact words.

Punctuation marks are signals, too. They signal different kinds of sentences and tell the reader when to pause or stop. Punctuation marks help writers organize their words so that the meaning is clear.

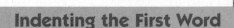

Indenting the First Word

The **first word** of a paragraph is indented, or moved in. Begin the first word about three spaces in from the left margin.

> The last day of school is fun. We turn in our books, and then we play games. We are sad, too. We must say good-bye to our teacher.

Period

A **period** means "stop." Periods signal the end of a sentence, an abbreviation, or an initial. They are also used after the numbers and letters in an outline.

> **Remember:**
> Use a capital letter to begin a sentence and a period to end it.

⭐ **To End a Sentence**

A **period** is used at the end of a sentence that tells something.

statement: Today is the last day of school.
I'm glad summer is here.

A **period** is also used at the end a sentence that tells someone to do something.

command: Don't be late for dinner.
Close the door when you leave.

★ **In Titles and Abbreviations**

Use a period after each **initial** of a person's name.

> Thomas A. Edison
>
> J. Edgar Hoover
>
> R. L. Stevenson

Use a period at the end of **an abbreviation of a title.**

> Gen. Colin Powell
>
> Mrs. Roosevelt
>
> Dr. Jonas Salk
>
> Douglas Fairbanks, Sr.

Also use a period at the end of **abbreviations for days and months.**

Monday	Mon.	January	Jan.
Tuesday	Tues.	February	Feb.
Wednesday	Wed.	March	Mar.

★ **In Outline Form**

Use periods when you list items in an **outline**. Add a period after the Roman numerals (I, II, III) that show the main topics. Add a period after the capital letters that list the facts supporting the main topic.

> Maya Lin—Architect

main topic: I. Designed Public Memorials

facts: A. Vietnam Veterans Memorial in Washington, D.C.

B. Civil Rights Memorial in Montgomery, Alabama

A **question mark** is used at the end of a sentence that asks a question. It lets the reader know that the sentence is asking for an answer.

How many days does July have?

Is January the first month of the year?

Did you answer all the questions?

When can we go?

Who will be there?

An **exclamation point** is used at the end of a sentence to show strong feelings. It can signal excitement, joy, fear, pain, or surprise.

Look, there's a whale!

I have a new baby brother!

Don't move!

Ouch!

Happy New Year!

Remember:
Different kinds of punctuation help make your writing interesting.

What?

Wow!

Cool!

A **comma** is used to keep words and ideas from running together. Commas help make writing easier to read.

★ **With City and State**

Use a comma to separate the names of a city and state.

city and state: My best friend moved to Las Vegas, Nevada.

★ **With City and Country**

Use a comma to separate the names of a city and a country.

city and country: He was born in Sydney, Australia.

Remember:

Don't use a comma between the state name and the ZIP code.

★ **In Addresses**

Use a comma to separate the parts of an address.

I live at 74 Park Street, Los Angeles, California 91301.

★ **In Dates**

Use a comma to separate the parts of a date.

in a date: August 19, 1999

in a sentence: I moved to New Jersey on Monday, May 23, 1995.

★ In Greeting of a Letter

Use a comma after the **greeting** of a friendly letter.

> Dear Grandma and Grandpa,

★ In Closing of a Letter

Use a comma after the **closing** of a friendly letter or business letter.

> Love,   Yours truly,

★ With Numbers

Use commas to keep long numbers clear.

> They traveled 2,000 miles to see us!
>
> Their car has 133,000 miles on it.
>
> Grandpa wants to sell it for $1,200.

Do not use a comma to separate numbers in years.

> My grandfather was born in 1942.

★ In Compound Sentences

Use a comma before the conjunction when it is used to join two complete sentences into a compound sentence. Do not use a comma if a conjunction joins two sentence parts.

> Dad stopped the car. Andy got in the back.
>
> Dad stopped the car, and Andy got in the back.

> I like swimming. I like soccer better.
>
> I like swimming, but I like soccer better.

Remember:
A compound sentence is two simple sentences joined together.

★ In a Series

Words in a **series** is a list of three or more things. Use commas to separate items in a series.

> Cats, dogs, and rabbits are my favorite pets.

> We worked, played, and slept.

★ After Introductory Words

Use a comma after words like *Yes* and *No* when they begin a sentence.

> Yes, I can ride a bike.

> No, I can't stay.

Use a comma to set off the name of a person spoken to.

> Alan, be careful!

> Janet, come to dinner.

★ After Phrases

A **phrase** is a group of words. Use a comma to set off a phrase that begins a sentence.

> Once upon a time, a kind giant lived in our land.

> After many years, the giant suddenly left.

★ With Direct Quotations

Use a comma to set off a person's exact words from the rest of the sentence.

> "The early bird gets the worm" is an old saying.

> Grandmother said, "A stitch in time saves nine."

Underlining or **italics** *(slanted type)* is used to identify the titles of books, plays, movies, and television programs.

A handwritten title should be underlined. A title written on a computer should appear in italics.

by hand: My favorite book is <u>Ramona Forever</u>.

by computer: My favorite book is *Ramona Forever*.

Remember:
Give your stories titles that will catch a reader's attention.

An **apostrophe** (') shows that letters have been left out of a word. It can also be used to show that something belongs to someone.

★ **In Contractions**

A **contraction** is a short word made from two other words. Use an apostrophe to show where one or more letters have been left out.

two words:	did not	they are	it is
contraction:	didn't	they're	it's

★ **With Possessive Nouns**

Use an apostrophe or *'s* to show that something belongs to someone.

singular noun: My coach's rules are fair.

plural noun ending in *s*: The girls' team won.

plural noun not ending in *s*: The men's team lost.

Use **quotation marks** (" ") to show the exact words of a speaker. Quotation marks are also used with certain kinds of titles.

★ **In Conversation**

Use quotation marks before and after a speaker's exact words. Write the punctuation mark that ends the speaker's words *inside* the quotation mark.

> "What time is it?" asked the child.
>
> "It is past your bedtime!" replied Dad.
>
> "I'm not sleepy," said the child.

★ **With Titles of Stories and Poems**

Use quotation marks before and after the titles of stories, poems, and other short works.

short story:	"Why Mosquitoes Fly"
poem:	"River Is a Piece of Sky"
article:	"Talking About Pets"
song:	"The Wheels on the Bus"

Remember:
When you write a conversation, start a new paragraph each time the speaker changes.

Neat handwriting and good penmanship are important. If your handwriting is neat and clear, your paper will be easier to read. Readers can focus on what you're saying.

Handwriting

When you write a final copy of a letter, article, or story, be sure to write neatly and clearly. The chart shows the correct way to form capital and lowercase letters.

a b c d e f g h i j k l m n
o p q r s t u v w x y z
A B C D E F G H I J K L M
N O P Q R S T U V W X Y Z

Remember:
Neatness counts.

a b c d e f g h i j k l m n
o p q r s t u v w x y z
A B C D E F G H I J K L M
N O P Q R S T U V W X Y Z

Format

How your final copy looks is important, too. It should be neat and clean. Try not to make smudges or cross out too many words. If necessary, make a new final draft.

Use lined paper and keep the margins the same. Leave one inch on the top, sides, and bottom of your paper.

Indent the first line of every paragraph. Sometimes your teacher may want you to write on every other line on your paper so it is easier to read and correct.

Syllables

Writers know how important it is to spell words correctly. Misspelled words can make the writer's meaning unclear.

Use a dictionary if you are not sure of how to spell a word. If you don't have a dictionary handy, remember that many words follow a few simple spelling patterns or rules.

Dividing a word into syllables can help you spell it. There is one syllable for each vowel sound. Say a word and count the vowel sounds to find the number of syllables in the word.

Closed Syllables

A **closed syllable** ends in one or more consonants.

hat   hand   bet   bit

In a word that has two closed syllables, a consonant from each syllable separates the vowels.

rab•bit   nap•kin

Open Syllables

An **open syllable** ends in a vowel sound rather than a consonant sound.

ra•dar   pi•lot   mo•tor   li•on

Remember:
Syllables can help you say and spell new words.

Vowels can be long or short. A short vowel usually comes between two consonants. A long vowel has the same sound as its letter name.

Many one-syllable words have **short vowel** sounds. The vowel comes between two consonants. Spell these sounds with one letter.

SHORT VOWEL SOUNDS				
Sounds	Letters	Words		
short a	a	flag	grab	track
short e	e	belt	sent	stem
short i	i	fist	grin	pinch
short o	o	clock	log	stop
short u	u	club	dust	luck

Remember:
Say the word aloud to hear the vowel sound clearly.

Many short vowels follow the consonant-vowel-consonant pattern, but others do not.

SHORT VOWEL SOUNDS				
Sound	Letters	Words		
short a	a-e	dance		
short e	ea, ai	weather	said	
short i	y, i-e	myth	lived	
short o	a	wander		
short u	o, ou, o-e	mother	country	come

Long Vowels

A **long vowel** sounds like its name. If a word ends in *e* after the final consonant, the vowel is usually long.

Adding an *e* to the end of each word makes the vowel sound long.

bit + e = bite

cap + e = cape

cut + e = cute

hop + e = hope

pet + e = Pete

Remember:
A long vowel says its name. A short vowel does not.

★ Letter Combinations

Long vowel sounds are also spelled with two vowels. The first letter usually stands for the long sound. The second letter is silent.

LONG VOWEL SOUNDS			
Sound	Letters	Words	
long a	ai	paid	train
	ay	say	stay
long e	ea	dream	mean
	ey	key	money
long i	ie	lie	pie
long o	oa	float	road
	ow	low	window
long u	ew	few	flew
	ue	due	Tuesday

An ending is a letter or group of letters added at the end of a word. Writers add endings to words to make a word singular or plural or to tell when an action happened.

endings   **s**   **es**   **ed**   **ing**

Words That End With a Consonant

If a word ends in a consonant, do not change the spelling of the word before adding *s, ed,* or *ing.*

Word	s	ed	ing
help	helps	helped	helping
start	starts	started	starting

Adding es

Add *es* to verbs that end in *ss, sh, ch, x,* or *zz* to make them plural. Do not change the spelling to add *ed* or *ing.*

Word	es	ed	ing
dress	dresses	dressed	dressing
crash	crashes	crashed	crashing
pitch	pitches	pitched	pitching
mix	mixes	mixed	mixing

Remember:
When you change the ending of a noun or verb, make sure the subject and verb agree.

Endings

Words That End With e

If a word ends in silent *e*, drop the *e* before adding *es*, *ed*, or *ing*.

Word	es	ed	ing
love	loves	loved	loving
smile	smiles	smiled	smiling

Words That End With y

If a word ends in a consonant and *y*, change the *y* to *i* and add *es* or *ed*.

Word	es	ed
family	families	
hurry	hurries	hurried
carry	carries	carried

Do not change *y* to i when you add *ing*.

carry   carrying
hurry   hurrying

If a word ends in a vowel and *y*, add only the ending.

stay   stays   stayed   staying
day   days

Double the Final Consonant

For most one-syllable words that end in a vowel and a consonant, double the final consonant when adding *ed* or *ing*.

pat   patted   patting

A **prefix** is a group of letters added to the beginning of a root, or base word. It forms a new word with a new meaning.

Do not change the spelling of the base word when you add a prefix.

prefix	+	base word	=	new word
dis	+	appear	=	disappear
un	+	happy	=	unhappy

These are some common prefixes and their meanings.

Adding Prefixes		
Prefix	Meaning	New Word
pre	**before**	**preschool**
re	**again**	**rewrite**
im	**not**	**impossible**
non	**not**	**nonstop**
ex	**out of, from**	**exit**
un	**not**	**unsure**
tri	**three**	**tricycle**
dis	**the opposite of**	**disobey**

Remember:
A prefix added to the beginning of a word does not change the spelling of the main word.

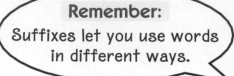

Suffixes

A **suffix** is a group of letters added at the end of a root, or base word. Use suffixes to change how a word is used in a sentence.

To add most suffixes, follow the same rules used to add endings.

▶ For help with adding endings, see pages 265 and 266.

Remember:
Suffixes let you use words in different ways.

Suffix	Meaning	New Word
ion	state of	inspection, decision
ment	result	movement
ness	state of	kindness
ful	full of	careful
less	without	hopeless
ly	in some way	easily
able	able to be	readable

A **root**, or base word, is the main part of a word. Prefixes, suffixes, and endings may be added to a root. Adding word parts to roots forms new words with new meanings.

read   reader   readable

reading   rereading   unreadable

Some Common Roots: drink   read   speak   happy

Do not change the spelling of the root when adding a prefix in front of it.

un   +   happy   =   unhappy

When adding a **suffix** or **ending** to a root, check for spelling changes. Use the spelling rules you already know.

In some words, you can't hear a final vowel sound. Instead, you hear a *schwa sound*. The word *pencil* has the *schwa l sound*. The word *taken* has the *schwa n sound*. Schwa sounds can be spelled different ways.

Schwa l	schwa n
pickle	eleven
tunnel	season
evil	captain
central	woman

Remember:
Knowing the root or base word can help you figure out the meaning of a new word.

Compound Words

A **compound word** is made of two or more words used together as a new word.

sun	+	shine	=	sunshine
water	+	fall	=	waterfall
out	+	side	=	outside
sea	+	shell	=	seashell
post	+	card	=	postcard

Homonyms

Homonyms are words that sound alike. Writers are careful when they use homonyms because the words have different meanings and different spellings. Be sure to use the spelling and meaning that's right for the sentence.

★ **hair/hare**　Wash your hair with that new shampoo.

A hare is an animal that's larger than a rabbit.

★ **bare/bear**　He put his bare feet on the cold floor and shivered.

A brown bear lives in the woods.

★ **pear/pair**　I ate a yellow pear.
I borrowed a pair of skates.

★ **hear/here**　We can hear the thunder.
Carry the table over here.

Some homonyms cause problems because they sound the same but have different meanings and spellings.

★ **you're/your**

contraction	You're (you are) late again.
possessive pronoun	Where is your late pass?

★ **our/hour**

possessive pronoun	Our soccer team always wins.
noun	They practice for an hour.

★ **they're/their/there**

contraction	They're (they are) home!
possessive pronoun	The girls took off their coats.
adverb	We live there.

Remember:
Use an apostrophe when you write a contraction.

★ **it's/its**

contraction	It's (it is) cold outside.
possessive pronoun	The bear sleeps in its den.

Synonyms and Antonyms

A **synonym** is a word that has the same or almost the same meaning as another word.

big/large   happy/glad   fast/quick

An **antonym** is a word that is opposite or almost opposite in meaning.

large/small   empty/full   light/dark

Using a Dictionary

A **dictionary** is one of the handiest books a writer can use. It tells what words mean, how they are spelled, and how to pronounce them.

Entry Words

The words in a dictionary appear in alphabetical order, beginning with *A* and ending with *Z*. Here is a sample. The word in dark type is the entry word.

denim (den´im) n. a coarse cotton cloth that is very strong and does not wear out easily. It is used for work clothes or play clothes.

den•im   n.

Beside the entry word are letters that tell you how to pronounce the word. The *n.* that follows tells you that the word is a noun. The definition, or meaning, is next. The end line shows how to divide the word into syllables.

Remember:
You can find all sorts of interesting information and facts in a dictionary.

Guide Words

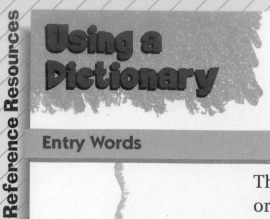

At the top of every dictionary page is a pair of **guide words** like the ones below.

rake   rank

These words tell you that the first word on this page is **rake** and the last word is **rank**. Any word that comes after **rake** and before **rank** in alphabetical order will be on this page.

Each entry word in the dictionary has a respelling that shows how to pronounce the word. The **pronunciation key** lists the symbols used to respell a word.

Each letter or symbol in the key stands for only one sound. This sound is shown in the word that follows the symbol, called the **key word**.

Remember:
Use the sounds in key words to help sound out words in the dictionary.

a cat	ō go	u fur	ə = a *in* ago
ā ape	ô law, for	ch chin	e *in* agent
ä cot, car	͝oo look	sh she	i *in* pencil
e ten	o͞o tool	th thin	o *in* atom
ē me	oi oil	*th* then	u *in* circus
i fit	ou out	zh measure	
ī ice	u up	ŋ ring	

To pronounce a word, find the symbols on the pronunciation key that match the letters in the respelling. Then sound out the word.

Dividing a Word Into Syllables

Both the respelling of an entry word and the end line of the entry show you how to **divide a word into syllables.** In the respelling, spaces separate the syllables. In the end line, dots separate the syllables.

Parts of Speech

Next, an abbreviation tells what **part of speech** the entry word is.

n.	**noun**	adv.	**adverb**
v.	**verb**	prep.	**preposition**
pron.	**pronoun**	conj.	**conjunction**
adj.	**adjective**	interj.	**interjection**

Word Meanings

The main purpose of a dictionary is to give the meaning of the word. When a word has more than one meaning, the first definition given is usually the most common one.

entry word

pronunciation

parts of speech

definitions

end line

syllable division

plural

sample sentence

E

eagle (ē′gəl) *n.* a large, strong bird of prey that has sharp eyesight.
ea·gle ■ *n., plural* **eagles**

ear¹ (ir) *n.* **1** either one of the two organs in the head with which a human being or an animal hears sounds. **2** the part of the ear that sticks out from the head. **3** the sense of hearing [She has a good *ear* for music.]
ear ■ *n., plural* **ears**

ear² (ir) *n.* the part of a cereal plant on which the seeds grow [an *ear* of corn].
ear ■ *n., plural* **ears**

eardrum (ir′drum) *n.* the thin, tight skin that is stretched inside the ear. It vibrates when sound waves strike it.
ear·drum ■ *n., plural* **eardrums**

Earhart (er′härt), **Amelia** (ə mēl′yə) 1898-1937; early U.S. airplane pilot who set records for long-distance flying.
Ear·hart, A·mel·i·a

earl (url) *n.* a British nobleman.
earl ■ *n., plural* **earls**

early (ur′lē) *adv.* **1** near the beginning of something; soon after the start [He won great fame *early* in his career.] **2** before the usual or expected time [The bus arrived *early*.]
adj. **1** near the beginning of something; soon after the start [We ate in the *early* afternoon.] **2** happening, coming, or appearing before the usual or expected time [an *early* spring].
ear·ly ■ *adv.* ■ *adj.* **earlier, earliest**

earmuffs (ir′mufs) *pl.n.* a pair of cloth or fur coverings that are worn over the ears to keep them warm.
ear·muffs ■ *pl.n.*

earn (urn) *v.* **1** to get as pay for work that has been done [She *earns* $10 an hour.] **2** to get or deserve because of something done [He *earned* a medal for swimming.]
earn ■ *v.* **earned, earning**
● The words **earn** and **urn** sound alike.
How much money do you *earn* in a year?
The museum has a Greek *urn* collection.

earnest (ur′nəst) *adj.* serious or sincere; not light or joking [It is my *earnest* wish that you will go to college.]
ear·nest ■ *adj.*

sounds to the ear from a radio, telephone, hearing aid, or other apparatus. An earphone is held to the ear or placed in the ear.
ear·phone ■ *n., plural* **earphones**

earring (ir′iŋ) *n.* a piece of jewelry that is a decoration for the lobe of the ear.
ear·ring ■ *n., plural* **earrings**

earth (urth) *n.* **1** the planet that we live on. It is the fifth largest planet and the third in distance away from the sun. **2** the dry part of this planet's surface, which is not the sea. **3** the soft, crumbly layer of the land's surface; soil or ground [The clay pot is filled with good, rich *earth*.]
—**down to earth** practical or sincere.

earring

earthen (urth′ən) *adj.* **1** made of earth [The hut had a hard *earthen* floor.] **2** made of baked clay [He carried water from the well in an *earthen* jar.]
earth·en ■ *adj.*

earthly (urth′lē) *adj.* **1** having to do with the earth, or life in this world, and not with the idea of a future life in heaven [She left all her *earthly* possessions to her children.] **2** possible [Your advice is of no *earthly* use.]
earth·ly ■ *adj.*

earthquake (urth′kwāk) *n.* a movement of the ground that feels like strong shaking or trembling. It is caused by shifts in rock underground or by the action of a volcano.
earth·quake ■ *n., plural* **earthquakes**

earthworm (urth′wurm) *n.* a worm that lives in the ground and helps to keep the soil loose.
earth·worm ■ *n., plural* **earthworms**

ease (ēz) *n.* **1** the condition of not having to try too hard [She swam a mile with *ease*.] **2** a calm or relaxed condition [She quickly put us at *ease*.] **3** the condition of being without worry, trouble, or need [They lived a life of *ease*.]

A thesaurus is like a dictionary. In addition to giving the meaning of words, it gives synonyms and antonyms. A thesaurus is very helpful when you're writing and need to find just the right word.

Like a dictionary, a thesaurus has entries that are listed in alphabetical order. Each entry word has a label that shows the part of speech. After this label is a list of synonyms, or words with similar meanings. This list is in alphabetical order.

entry word

part of speech

synonyms in alphabetical order

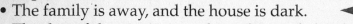

dark *adj.* dim, gloomy, murky, somber
These words share the meaning "having little or no light."
- The family is away, and the house is dark.
- The day of the picnic turned out dim and cloudy.
- Thousands of bats flew around in the gloomy cave.
- The cabin stands next to the murky pond.
- The living room is somber and depressing.
antonym: light

definition

sample sentences

antonym

Usually, one of the synonyms in the thesaurus entry will be just the word you need. Test the synonym by trying it out in your sentence. It should sound right and make sense.

Remember:
Keep your dictionary and thesaurus handy when you're writing.

Index